Pat Ingoldsby

is a poet, playwright, humourist and broadcaster of national repute. His live performances in theatres and art centres throughout the country are immensely popular. Eight collections of Pat's best-selling poetry have been published. His radio plays have been broadcast at home and abroad. This is his first prose book, drawn from articles which first appeared in the *Evening Press*. Extracts from this book have been included in Ferdia MacAnna's *The Anthology of Irish Comic Writing*.

Other books by Pat Ingoldsby

POETRY
You've Just Finished Reading This Title
Rhyme Doesn't With Reason
Up The Leg Of Your Jacket
Welcome To My Head (Please Remove Your Boots)
Salty Water
Scandal Sisters
How Was It For You Doctor
Poems So Fresh And So New

FOR CHILDREN
Zany Tales
Tell Me A Story Pat (audio cassette)

The
Peculiar
Sensation
of Being
Irish

Pat Ingoldsby

Killeen

First published in October 1995 by
Killeen
an imprint of
Three Spires Press,
Killeen,
Blackrock Village,
Cork City,
Ireland.

The articles in this book originally
appeared in *The Evening Press*, Dublin.
They have been selected and arranged by
Pat Cotter

ISBN 1-873548-31-1

Cover design: Pat Cotter\Upper Case
Cover photo: Liz Twomey
Typesetting: Three Spires Press
Printed in Ireland by Colour Books

For
Rory Gallagher
"Lone Warrior"
Thank you for the music.

Contents

First Two Pieces With Absolutely No Laughs Whatsoever

The Government is in charge of this country. So I am writing this letter to our Government. Dear Government, It was lashing rain today. It was also very cold. I saw at least three of this nation's children sitting on the pavement. They were begging. I pass through Dublin city centre two or three times every day. There are always young children sitting on the ground with their hands outstretched . These children are being robbed of their childhood. They have got the same human rights as every other child in this land. Yet they are being forced to sit out in the bitter cold and ask passers-by for a bit of change. This is grievously wrong. I am asking you to act immediately. I am asking you to put a stop to it right away. Please do something now. We keep saying what a terrible shame it is and we keep saying that it shouldn't be allowed. But day after day the children are still there. One of the girls I saw in O'Connell Street today had a very bad cough. She was crying. If I was forced to stand out in the freezing cold and rain like she was, I would be crying too. Will you please consider appointing a Minister for Children's Rights? There are some terrible things being done to children in Ireland. Some of them are afraid to go to school. They waken up in the morning with a sick feeling of fear in their stomachs. I know that the Minister for Education is doing her best to tackle the problem of bullying. But this Minister has got lots of other problems on her plate as well. I'm not sure which minister is working on the horror of child sex abuse. But I think that the time is right for you to appoint a special minister with total responsibility for all of our children. Someone who can make sure that none of our young people are denied the precious gift of a childhood full of joy and wonder. The unfortunate children who are forced to beg on our streets have got nobody to speak out on their behalf. God alone knows how they must be feeling. They are so conditioned to ask for money that no matter what you say to them, they usually reply by asking you for a bit of change. You are in charge of this country. Our children are very special citizens. They deserve better than a life of begging. Please raise this most important of matters in the Dail. Please put an end to this shameful exploitation of our most vulnerable citizens.

Please do it without delay.

You owe it to our nation's children.

The Pavement Is Cold And Hard

20.25pm: The young woman was sitting on the path against a wall in Temple Bar, begging for a bit of help. She told me that she was begging on O'Connell Bridge a couple of weeks ago. It was seven o'clock in the evening. A young well-dressed guy climbed up onto the parapet near to her and sat on it. Then he deliberately toppled backwards into the river. She tried to get help. She tried to stop a succession of passers-by, but none of them would stop because she was a traveller. They just kept walking. When she eventually got someone to listen they sent for an ambulance and they got the young man out of the river. She didn't say whether he was alive or dead. Perhaps she didn't know.

21.05pm An old woman was sitting in a shop doorway in Grafton Street. Her face was bruised. She asked me for a smoke so I gave her the packet. She put her hand in underneath her coat and produced a radio which she gave to me. She kept insisting that I take it but it didn't seem right to walk away with a good radio in exchange for a pack of cigarettes.   I asked her why she didn't want it and she said that she didn't have any batteries. I told her to hang on in the doorway while I went up the street to a shop and got some for her. On the way up I passed a couple of Gardai on foot-patrol heading down towards the doorway. The shop didn't have any batteries. When I got back to the doorway the old woman was gone.

21.30. The young man said he was sixteen. He was bright, articulate, smiling and homeless. He knows where the good squats are. He has worked out a way of living for himself which includes regular showers, clean clothes and keeping one step ahead of trouble. When he was fourteen he was living in a hostel for homeless boys. Then the hostel closed and everyone was moved out. He used his wits and moved back in again so that he had free electricity and central heating for a while. He said that when he's eighteen he hopes to go to America and see what the story is over there.

22pm. A man wrapped in a blanket called me over in Dame Street. He said that he wished to share some of his wisdom with me. He had written it down on a page torn out of a copybook. All about the way we often make the mistake of pre-judging people by their appearance. People are always doing it to him because he wanders the streets at night with a blanket around him.

22.30pm. I'm sitting in Rumpoles Bar listening to Parchman Farm playing the blues. The man in the blanket is outside the window and he's dancing very happily to the music. His wisdom is tucked away safely underneath his blanket.

Run For Cover When Compliments Fly

I received an Irish compliment yesterday. "I heard one of your little poems on the radio last week . . . by accident. And I have to give you this much — you do amuse me occasionally." We have got such a lovely way of paying somebody a compliment and leaving them feeling totally shafted. The opening expression says it all. "I have to give you this much." In other words, I am now going to tell you something good about yourself, I don't find this easy, I intend to dilute it as much as possible because I don't want you getting a swelled head about yourself, God knows you're bad enough as it is, but what the hell, you do have your moments.

Some people prefer to deliver the sting at the very beginning. "I have to be honest with you. I used to think that you hadn't got a thought in your head. In fact, I used to say to the wife —That guy should be locked away for the common good." And you stand there waiting for the good bit. It's always a long time coming. When someone announces that they are going to be honest with you and tell you all the things they used to think, it's time to run for cover. They give you the lot. All the times they switched you off, all the times you came between them and their dinner, all the times they nearly put their foot through the television. By the time they reach the compliment you have really earned it. "No, I mean, fair is fair ... I have to admit it. You mightn't be the best of them but then again you're not the worst." That's about as good as it's going to get.

Taking the wind out of famous sails is a national pastime. "I ran into Bono yesterday and my God I wish you'd been there because I told him ...you should have heard me ...oh I told him all right." Our mission in life seems to be the dishing out of home truths. "I met your man last week ... him with his big car but don't worry. I reminded him about the time he didn't have an arse in his trousers." It seems to be very important to us in Ireland to remind people about their arseless trousers. An aged aunt of mine used to go one better. Every time she saw a photograph of Sean T. O'Ceallaigh, *Uachtaran na h-Eireann* in the paper she would snort triumphantly ..."I used to live next door to that man — I saw him putting his bin out every Tuesday." Nobody is safe. If they don't get you by the trousers they'll get you by the bin.

*

I think that we are very bad at saying good things to one another. We seem to find it so much easier to put someone down than to build them up. I was having a lovely chat with an old man yesterday. A woman who was walking past looked at both of us and then said to me — "I see you're keeping very bad company today." And she laughed.

We always laugh when we come out with something like that. We can always cover ourselves by saying — "Sure I was only joking." Too many of our jokes seem to involve diminishing other people. As a nation we have brought the put-down remark to a fine art.

I was putting a packet of frozen chicken into my supermarket trolley yesterday. A woman who I have never seen before in my life was walking past. Without a moment's hesitation she said —"They're bad for you." And she walked on. I wouldn't like to be married to her very much.

I was first into the swimming pool and was floating on my back and happily singing away to myself. The next person into the pool was a woman who moved past me in the water. Straight away she said to me — "Anybody can sing in the bath." I think it's a great pity that we go through life saying things like that to one another.

We are not used to receiving compliments. I told a man how brilliant he was looking yesterday and he paused. And he waited. Then he asked — "Is that it?" So I nodded. He looked genuinely bewildered. "Eh-you're not going to say —'for your age' or something like that?" I shook my head.

"No — you look marvellous and that's it... nothing else except that I'm very happy to see you." He was still not convinced. "Eh — you're not looking for something, are you?" Our meeting would have been a lot less complicated if I had simply greeted him with — "There you are — still looking as diabolical as ever." He would have had no trouble at all about handling that.

We concentrate daily on not giving one another a swollen head. I was standing in a bus queue reading the morning paper when a man who I know reasonably well greeted me with the words — "Still pretending we can read the written word are we Ingoldsby?" I think we talk to one another like this because we don't like ourselves very much. So we try to ensure that other people don't like themselves very much either.

As long as we believe the old saying — "Self-praise is no praise" I think that we have still got a very long way to go towards basic self-esteem.
*

There's Asking In The Telling

I'm not mad about statements which are really questions in disguise. "I don't see you on the television at all this weather." On the face of it, that seems to be a person telling me something. Hidden just below the surface are built-in questions like - "Were you fired or what?" ... "Is there something that we don't know about?" ... "How are you paying your ESB bills now?" I moved house last year. A lot of people told me that since. "I see you've moved house then." Translation — "Where are you living now?" A lot more people have told me where I'm not living now. "You're not down on the seafront anymore." I bloody well know that. "You've got another place so." Translation — "Did you have to move or what?"

You'll get the next one when you walk into a small pub down the country. "I'd say you're not from around these parts." Everybody in the place knows that already and so do you. A lovely way to snooker the hidden question is simply one delicious word. "Correct." Say it in a quiet, friendly way. A magnificent uneasy silence follows. You can hear the clock ticking. A hidden question has just bitten the dust.

Time the silence with your watch. The longest I've ever managed is one minute. 27 seconds. That was when someone else tried a follow-up statement. "I'd say you've travelled a long way all the same." Go for your second snooker.
"I thought you said you'd be here at two thirty." That one is a real beauty. You are actually being asked — "What the hell kept you?" Torpedo the hidden question by responding to the statement. "You're absolutely right, I did." The confused silence will be so loud that you could almost record it. People love telling you what they don't see. "I don't see you down the other place much this weather" . . . "I don't see your brother and his wife out together much these days" . . . "I don't see whatshisname at Mass anymore." Translation — "If you know something about it that I don't, you can tell me even though I'm not actually asking you." "Long time no see." Translation — "I haven't seen you anywhere for ages so you owe me a full explanation." The hell you do. You can swing this one around in seconds with — "Come to think of it — I haven't seen YOU for an awful long time." Put a little hint of accusation into it. If you get it right, the other person now feels obliged to do all the explaining. Proper order.
*

You Never Used To Talk Like That

It's funny the way that some people change their voices. I know at least two people who used to have lovely musical country accents. It was a joy to listen to them. Then they came to Dublin. They moved very gradually from bedsit, to flat, to apartment.

They turned left at the signpost marked "Towards the In Crowd" and that's where we lost touch with one another.   I bumped into each of them again during the year. They have both undergone voice and accent transplants. They now use the letter "o" where lesser mortals use an "a". If you break your leg you are fitted with a "ploster cost". If you travel up North you must visit "Belfost".   They also put in an "e" where non-glitterati used an "a". As far as most of us are concerned "The cat sat on the mat in the flat." Cats have been doing this for years. Substitute the letter "e" and suddenly the unfortunate "pussy cet set on the met in the flet". How people can talk like this with a straight face is beyond me.

Sometimes I find the news on the radio very confusing. Not so long ago a newsreader said that a hospital patient had just undergone a "transplont". I rushed to my dictionary to discover that a "tron" is 'a public weighing machine used also as a place of punishment, as by nailing the ear'. I couldn't find a "plont" anywhere. Perhaps this was just as well.   I imagine that somewhere in Dublin is a textbook which contains posh little conversation pieces which you can practise daily in the privacy of your bathroom.   Lesson One: "Actually they removed his ploster cost and gave him a transplont, after which he returned to his flet where he was very heppy to discover that his cet was still sitting on the met." The correct response to every sentence of this nature is: "Absolutely!"

This sort of language can be baffling for beginners. A golfer playing a post stroke — on the green uses his "patter". The actual stroke is called a "patt". Yet if the golfer's name happens to be Pat he is now called "Pet". "Pet played a very good patt." The golf course in question can be either in "Dablin" or "Belfost".   I think we should all go back to speaking in Irish.
*

Bats And Garlic

If you are planning your summer holidays in Transylvania there are some very important things you need to remember. The villagers in the foothills know exactly what they are talking about. Listen to them. If they warn you not to go anywhere near the castle up on the mountain for God's sake do as they say.

If they huddle together in little frightened groups and fill their bedrooms with garlic, they have a perfectly good reason. If they speak in whispers and keep making the Sign of the Cross, they know precisely what they are at. Get onto the first bus out of there and don't get off it until you reach a country whose name doesn't end with 'vania'. Do not wander into the forest. Better people than you have gone in to look at the primroses and they have never done the Lotto again. If you find yourself stranded in a clearing for some unavoidable reason, like your helicopter making a forced landing, do the sensible thing. Climb up the nearest tree, make a cross with two twigs and stay there until help arrives from the local monastery. A black coach will come galloping along after about five minutes and will stop directly under your tree. You'll know it straight away because it won't have any driver. Then a thunderstorm will begin to rage around you and soak you to the skin. No matter how cold or miserable you are, DO NOT GET INTO THE COACH. You may find this hard to believe but every year countless travellers sit into the driverless coach and off they go at a mad gallop up the mountain with thunder crashing all around them. The villagers have warned them 'till they're blue in the face but it never makes a blind bit of difference. Your travel insurance will not cover you for bites on your neck and all your blood gone. If you find yourself standing outside the castle in a raging storm, your insurance company won't want to know about it. It's no use explaining that the door opened and a wizened butler in black said, "Come in . . . my master is expecting you." Insurance companies are browned off with people who wander into strange castles full of cobwebs and get their necks bitten. As far as they are concerned you should have known better and I am inclined to agree with them. Never mind the fact that there was a place set for you at the table. That is no excuse. If you choose to sit down to a bowl of soup with bats whizzing around your head,-you deserve everything you get.

Garlic butter tastes lovely on Chicken Kiev but that is a different thing altogether.

*

Brown Bread And Vikings

I never mean to tell lies to tourists. It's just that I see them reading plaques on old buildings and the writing on them isn't very interesting. So I think of good things to tell them in order to put a bit of jizz into their holidays.

The American tourists in Glendalough were delighted when I told them about the Vikings trying to capture the monks' recipe for brown bread. We were standing together looking up at the round tower when I explained about St. Kevin and his followers baking the bread all day and praising God.

"The Vikings would be sitting in their long boats off Ireland's Eye doing crosswords and learning Irish phrases when the appetising aroma of freshly-baked brown bread would be wafted towards them on the wind."

One American woman wanted to know if they made soda bread as well, so I told her that the recipe for that belonged to the monks out on the Aran Islands

"If the wind was in the right direction, the Vikings smelt that as well, so they would send one of their boats off towards Galway while the rest of them took off across country to Glendalough."

It's quite extraordinary how a story like that takes on a momentum of its own and suddenly all the monks are scrambling up a ladder into the round tower with the recipe for brown bread written just like the Book of Kells on ancient parchment. Meanwhile the Vikings are down below trying to think of ways to coax the monks out.

One American called Henry suggested starving them out, but his wife looked at him with scorn. "Those guys would have rooms full of brown bread up there, Henry — the whole tower was probably bursting with the stuff."

"And home-made butter," suggested a woman called Martha.

"And mead," said her sister. "Don't forget the mead."

We stood there in a little group looking up at a tower full of monks and brown bread and we racked our brains for some way of getting them down.

"I suppose," said Martha, "you could always say in a very loud voice — 'OK, boys ... let's all go over to the Aran Islands to get some soda bread!' Then you could pretend to go but you'd really hide in the bushes."

Henry was more in favour of psychological warfare. "How about building another round tower beside that one and all the Vikings climb into it and pull up the ladder and stay there? Now that would really confuse the monks."

I think I'll rewrite a few more plaques tomorrow. It's great for tourism.

*

Just How Green Are Their Valleys?

I thought there was a row going on. As I went up the stairs on the bus I could hear people shouting. I'm glad I didn't rush down to the driver and say, "Put your foot to the floor and don't stop for anything until we reach Store Street Garda Station. I'll stick my head out the window and make ambulance siren noises so you can hurtle through all the red lights." Two American tourist women were talking to each other in conversational shouts. Real top of the voice stuff. The way you'd talk if a hurricane was demolishing your house into crashing debris. I'd love to know why they do it   Suddenly things became dramatically worse. One of the women bellowed at an old man sitting across the aisle. "Are you Irish?" she roared. The man was very deaf. "I beg your pardon," he said. Oh God no, I thought. Now we're really going to get it. She jacked her voice up about 100 decibels and tried again. "ARE YOU IRISH!!?" "YES I AM!!" he replied with the sort of loud voice you use when you're listening to your Walkman. I do it myself whenever my hearing aid is temporarily out of action. I assume that the rest of the world is as bothered as myself.   "I JUST LOVE YOUR COUNTRY," she resonated, "IT'S SO EH..SO EH.." "NICE!!" roared the other woman. The old man thought for a moment. "IT'D BE GRAND IF IT WASN'T FOR THE WEATHER!!"

It'd be even grander, I thought, if you didn't come over here and talk at the top of your voices. Fair enough, our economy needs your dollars. But there's no need to shout. There's no need to talk to one another as if you're standing on opposite sides of The Curragh.   "NO! NO!" countered one of the American women. "YOUR WEATHER IS OK. IT'S OK BECAUSE IT MAKES EVERYTHING SO GREEN!"   I can never understand all this green stuff. Every year it's the same story.
People in check shirts and emerald peaked caps raving like visitors from another planet who have never set eyes on grass and trees and hedges before.   I've seen America in the films. Almighty God didn't leave them short. They've got tons and tons of lovely greenery. Mel Torme used to rave about the stuff. I've heard American tourists in England and Scotland. There's bloody fields and hedges all over the place. Yet they never yell at the natives about it. Why do they pick on us?   I think we should dye this whole country blue or purple.
*

My Dream-Holiday

I know exactly the kind of holiday that I would like. But unless I win billions of pounds I could never afford it. I want to spent one month cruising at sea on the QE2. But first of all I want to see a certificate which clearly states that the entire ship is free from feathers and housedust mite. I don't mind how long this takes because it will take me ages to save up the money. Then I want the QE2 placed in dry-dock so that they can convert it into a catfriendly environment. I want to bring Willow, Blackie and Hoot with me. I haven't had a holiday for nine years. They have never had one unless you count one week in the vets while I was in hospital last July.

I want all the dividing walls taken out over the full length of the ship. They can leave a few pillars standing up if they like, because the vessel would probably cave in without them.

Then a team of landscape gardeners can move in and recreate the area around my house. They can consult ordnance survey maps of all the back gardens in my neighbourhood and transform the full length of the QE2 into a perfect replica. Blackie, Willow and Hoot are used to rambling along the tops of garden walls and wriggling through hedges and they wouldn't really enjoy a Mediterranean cruise without them. Willow and Hoot are card-carrying tomcats. A very important part of their religion is making creative statements against trees and shrubs so we could have millions of them all along 'A' Deck. I don't mind other passengers travelling on the ship, but I would like the QE 2 people to check them out carefully in advance. Ideally they should be prepared to pay their fares in tins of Tuna Whiskas. If they have the slightest objection to fleas or essence of Hoot I would prefer them to get the car ferry and take a day trip to Holyhead or somewhere like that.

It shouldn't be too difficult to dismantle the hot-press from my house and re-assemble it on board. Whenever my cats are freaked by anything, that is where they hide. I once spent two very stressful days sailing through the Bay of Biscay and I wouldn't wish that sort of stormy trauma on anybody. So I want to be able to open the hot-press and say —"Right pussy cats … the next two days are going to be rough so inyou go." I might even join them myself.

I plan to walk into a Dublin travel agent's this week and ask for a preliminary quote. I think I'll go into Ray Treacy. It will take his mind off all this American visa stuff for a while.

*

Not-So-Hot Holiday Videos Of Our Time

People want action and movement in their holiday videos. This is why one of them holds the camera while their partner walks past things. If it's a famous monument they also pause, look up and point towards the top. "OK Martha … I want you to walk past the Eiffel Tower … not too fast now … about the same speed as Buckingham Palace." Martha knows how to pace herself. She doesn't start walking until Vernon shouts — "Go Martha Go!" Meanwhile, he is searching for the top of the tower in his viewfinder. Vernon realises that shots of Martha walking past famous monuments tend to lack dramatic interest. This is why he pans all the way down from the top to the bottom first. He knows that this creates unbearable tension. His family will sit at home during the winter in a fever of excitement. "My God—I wonder who Dad is going to find at the bottom of the Leaning Tower."

So far, Martha has walked past every famous monument of note from Boston to Bombay. On a shout of — "OK, pause, look up and point!"—she has done all three in the correct order. She has also stood alongside a bewildering assortment of London; policemen, Papal guards and French gendarmerie. They also go looking for inner city horses. "OK Martha—I've just panned along from the tail to the head. Start walking now! Right …that's great. Now pause, point and pat the head." It was in Rome that Martha dug in her heels. "Jeez, Vernon, I'm fed up walking past

things and pointing up. Why can't we do something different for a change?" This marks the point in their holiday videos where she begins to walk out of buildings.   "OK Martha —I want you to walk out of the Vatican. So just go into the hallway —right. Count backwards from twenty to one —this will give me time to pan down from the top to the bottom. Then   start walking." At any given moment during the summer an infinite number of Marthas are standing still in famous hallways and counting backwards. Meanwhile, their husbands are outside pointing video cameras up at the roof. Martha also walks towards tour buses, pauses, puts one foot onto the bottom step, turns and waves. She walks towards buskers, pretends to drop a coin into their guitar case, stands and listens.   Martha can't wait to get back home again. She won't have to walk past anything famous or point to the top of it for another glorious year.
*

A Trillion, Yes, But What's A Zillion?

The man said he hadn't got a clue. "A trillion? Don't ask me, Pat. I can tell you what a billion is all right ... but the trillion ... there I leave you." It's a new one on me as well. I was only starting to feel at home with the billion. Lots of people have told me the same thing. They were just starting to feel comfortable with it too. "Aw sure it'll probably cost a couple of billion or so ... not a bother."
The television newscaster sprang it on me last week. He said that Russia is looking for a loan of something like seven trillion. I can't even form a mental picture of it. How many suitcases full of money is that? Or are we talking about rooms? How many rooms stacked up to the ceiling?   The million just doesn't rate anymore. You can win that on the Lotto any day and you still couldn't afford to buy Tony Cascarino. No thank you very much-the million isn't worth the paper it's printed on. Sure it cost that much to put a new front onto the Abbey Theatre.

I read about some high-flyer In America who is down to his last three million and I actually feel sorry for the guy. I find myself thinking ... "God love him. ...there he is roughing it like the rest of us." I read about him being forced to sell off his private plane and two or three mansions and I have to stop myself from sending him on a few bob to tide him over until things pick up again.

I know what is going to happen. They are going to start sneaking the trillion up on us next. Give it two or three years and you won't bat an eyelid. "I hear that other thing over in Saudi cost a couple of trillion or so ... give or take a million ...you know yourself ... eh — two more pints and a small one there, Jerry."

I'm going to miss the million. You sort of got used to companies losing seven or eight of them in a year. "We wish to announce a trading loss of eight million pounds on our overseas operations for the past year. However, our loss for the previous year amounted to ten million so our present loss actually represents a net gain of two million." If you had done your sums that way in school you'd have been on the receiving end of a belt from the teacher.

My first job in insurance was looking after the petty cash. Five pounds in a green tin box. I was nearly fired when the float was fourpence short. I don't know why I bothered. You can lose a couple of million now during your lunch hour. Mark my words...the zillion will be next.

*

Talking To Your Handbag

It seems you've only got to put your handbag down for a second nowadays and it's gone. A lot of women have been telling me about thefts in pubs and restaurants. And I have been telling them that the time is absolutely right for a revolutionary new shouting handbag.

The idea couldn't be simpler. Your handbag is electronically programmed to respond to and recognise your touch. If you even tip it with your finger it whispers reassuringly — "Don't worry about a thing. I know it's you." If anybody else lays a hand on your bag it blasts out the opening chords of 'The 1812 Overture' and then yells at the top of its voice— "HARK AND HIST ! GET THY THIEVING HANDS OFF ME THOU NEFARIOUS BRIGAND !" That should do the trick. Nobody in their right mind is going to make off with a handbag which is roaring— "YE GODS ! I AM BEING ROBBED ! SOMEBODY SUMMON THE BOW STREET RUNNERS!"

I think that it's time for us to take a good look at burglar alarms as well because nobody takes a blind bit of notice anymore. People stroll past shops and houses at night and completely ignore flashing blue lights and ringing bells. The time is right for an alarm which makes the hair stand up on the back of your neck with a dramatic message: "DON'T JUST STAND THERE YOU UNRESPONSIVE PERSON ! I'M NOT SHOUTING AT YOU FOR THE GOOD OF MY HEALTH. RIGHT NOW MEN WITH BLACK MASKS AND STRIPY JUMPERS ARE PUTTING ALL THE BEST SILVER INTO SACKS MARKED 'SWAG'! IF YOU DON'T GO AND RING THE GUARDS THIS SECOND I'LL TAKE YOUR PHOTO AND GIVE IT TO MARION FINUCANE FOR HER 'CRIMELINE' PROGRAMME AND THEN WHERE WILL YOU BE?" It might be worth the idea of updating ambulance sirens while we're at it. The Minister for Health can record a terse message which can blare out from the top of the cab. "OUT OF THE WAY! I'M AN AMBULANCE AND IT COULD BE YOUR GRANNY WHO IS SICK SO MOVE OVER OR WE LL PUNCTURE YOUR TYRES WITH OUR DEADLY ACCURATE JAMES BOND ROCKETS!" They would only be pretend rockets but people needn't necessarily know that.

I for one would welcome the introduction of a discreet whispering zip or button fly. I don't do it on purpose but once again last week I wandered around the city centre for a full hour or so without any central defence whatsoever. Nobody breathed a

word to me about the presence of cheese on my chin or anything like that. Surely to goodness if a voice in your car can remind you to don your safety belt it would be just as easy for your jeans or trousers to whisper — "Pssst ! Gently pilgrim ... there is dairy produce on thy chin !" or anywhere else for that matter.
*

Hungry Tigers Make You Hasten

Miss Moore was absolutely right. I'd love to meet her again so that I could tell her that. When we were in third class, she told us about hungry tigers. She said that you never know how fast you can run until a hungry tiger comes after you. The thought sometimes occurred to me since that even if the tiger just had a five-course meal and was chasing you on a full stomach you would still fairly shift yourself.

Two guys demanded money from me last week. It was evening time on the North Circular Road. Still very bright. There was none of the usual, "Will you loan us a couple of pence?" It was more a case of, "Hand over the lot right now or you'll waken up with a crowd standing round you". I started to walk away very quickly. They followed me. I speeded up. So did they. Suddenly I was running with all the grace and artistry of a gazelle who has just copped on that he is about to be mugged by one of Miss Moore's tigers. My asthma simply seemed to vanish.

It's amazing the kind of thoughts which flash across your mind when you are whizzing along the North Circular Road with two hostile foes on your heels. I remember thinking, "This couldn't possibly be me because I can't run as fast as this." Then I speeded up a bit more and found myself thinking, "I wish that I'd brought my stopwatch with me because nobody will ever believe this." I started just past St. Peter's Church and finished up near St. Brendan's Hospital. I felt a glorious exhilaration when I finally shook them off. It was the kind of adrenaline charge you usually get after a good gig. My legs were still raring to go. "Come on Pat — how about Sligo and back while we're still in the mood?"

I can remember what the guys said to me when I told them that I wasn't going to give them any money. "You're on the television. You're loaded." There just wasn't time to explain that I gave all that up about three years ago. There wasn't time to say: "What you are proposing to do to me is very naughty — I'll tell your mammies and they will be really cross with you." It was a straightforward case of ' Hi Ho Silver' and away.

I prefer the Dublin children who tell you that they've just lost their bus fare. They never seem to do anything else. When you offer to help them look for it they explain that there isn't much point because they lost it in the Liffey. Nice and reasonable. There are no hungry tigers.

*

It was sticking out a mile that the guys were going to rob the bank. The townsfolk should have known. I mean when three mean-looking dudes ride their horses down the middle of main street and the music suddenly starts to go ... BONG ... BONG ...BONG...

The townsfolk in the old black and white westerns never seem to get the message. Fair enough ... they can't hear the BONG BONGS but you'd think they'd know all the same. The mean-looking dudes have got their eyes narrowed and they're wearing scruffy black hats and they're muttering to one another out of the sides of their mouths.

The townsfolk just keep on crossing the street and raising their hats to women in big bonnets and you want to yell at them — "Will you for God's sake go and get the sheriff, or better still, the marshal if you've got one."

In the last film that I saw, the mean-looking dudes walked into the bank and nobody froze or anything. It was patently obvious that they weren't going to lodge their pocket money or giro money to their mammies. If Roy Roger had been there he would have punched each one of them on the chin without making a loud punching noise and that would have been that.

But Roy was busy elsewhere talking to a newly born colt about how life can sometimes be tough but it's not really all that bad if you tell the truth all the time and raise your hat to old ladies in big bonnets.

Then the security guard in the bank recognised the three guys because he was secretly bad too, even though the bank manager didn't know that when he hired him. The guard was actually supposed to look the other way and do nothing. But one of Roy's previous homilies about respecting old men even though they spit out tobacco juice had obviously moved him very deeply.

Suddenly he picked up his rifle and shot the dudes, much to their surprise and annoyance . You could tell they were browned off about it by the way that they fell.

The bank manager seemed to take the whole thing very much in his stride. He simply stepped over the three inert forms on his floor and said to the guard: "I'll see that you get promotion and an annual increment for this." The townsfolk came out from behind barrels and started raising their hats and crossing the street again and life went on much as normal for a while.

They never seemed to know when the injuns were coming either. It's a miracle that any of them lived past the age of fifty.

*

Big Nixie Will Do Your Laundry For You

I would never steal loads of money. £2.5 million would take up an awful lot of space in your house. A taxi-man told me that it's a half a ton of paper. Where would you put it? I couldn't shove it in under the bed because I don't have one. After years of worrying about the bogey man grabbing me by the leg I now feel much safer sleeping on a mattress on the floor. It's brilliant because in the morning you simply roll out sideways and there's no way anybody can grab you.

God alone knows how you'd bring all that money to the bank. You'd have to borrow a street trader's pram and camouflage the top of it with bananas or Toblerone bars. God alone knows how you'd lodge it without causing suspicion.   They're used to me wandering into the bank with little bags of coins from my telephone bill flowerpot. I've got a separate flowerpot for my ESB bill. Once a week I put my coins into money bags and carry them down to the bank. No matter how casually I'd try to lodge £2.5 million in my current account they'd know bloody well that it didn't come out of my flowerpots. I could always lodge £100,000 at a time and say very casually that I've just had a good week at the poetry. But I have my doubts.

Winning the Lotto is a much better bet because they don't give you a half ton of paper. You get a handy little cheque which fits into your pocket.   I think you have to launder it when you rob a few million. I'm not too sure exactly what that means but they all seem to do it. I don't have any contacts and I'm not sure where you get in touch with them. I think that you go to a racetrack or a snooker hall and talk to people out of the side of your mouth. "Pssssst ...I need a bit of laundering done." Then they introduce you to "Big Nixie" or someone with a name like that and he does your laundry for you.   You wouldn't dare to put a small ad in the paper because no matter how carefully you worded it, someone would surely guess what you were up to. "Man seeks laundry service for half a ton of paper. Responsible rates." You'd never get away with it.

Swiss banks are all very well but not when you're scared stiff of flying. You'd have to travel overland which would take days. And a man trundling a pram covered with bananas on to the hovercraft would only draw unwanted attention to himself. I think I'll stick to my flowerpots. You don't have to disguise them with Toblerone bars or anything.

*

An Ecstacy Of Banks And Building Societies

I was half afraid to go into one building society. It was their poster on the bus shelter that did it. A huge big colour photo of five staff members looking out at me with enormous smiles on their faces. Written across the top in big letters was the message, "We Want To Talk To You." I would find that very hard to handle. My God— if I walked in off the street and the five of them were standing there grinning at me like that I know the first thing that I would do. I'd check my fly to make sure it wasn't open. I don't find it easy to talk to people who keep smiling all the time. I always think that they've got something to hide. Or they know something that I should know but they're not telling me. I saw an ad on television for another building society where a young couple are walking out of the manager's office. This is clearly the happiest moment of their whole lives. They are speechless with joy. I don't know what the pair of them were doing in there but it certainly seems to have made them very, very happy.

The manager is standing in his office doorway. His face is aglow with so much love and joy and caring that I watched and waited for him to be assumed into heaven. They probably couldn't do that bit in the ad because he would have gone straight up through the ceiling.

One of his female staff members is so delighted to see everyone else out of their heads with joy that you just know she wants to fling her folders up into the air and prance along the top of the counter. They're all at it. I saw an ad for a supermarket recently where they were all smiling and grinning and patting children on top of the head and I thought, "My goodness I'm never going in there either ... those people are clearly unbalanced." If someone is friendly by nature I don't believe that they need to advertise the fact. I would suspect anybody who feels the need to send me a smiling photo of themselves with the message "You're really going to like me." I went into a building society last month and said that I'd like to borrow £3,000 to publish my new book. The girl explained to me that I would have to get my house revalued and there would be fees to be paid and I would have to pay them and fair enough she was smiling but I wasn't. So I said thanks all the same and walked towards the door.   I half-thought about swinging around suddenly to see if everyone was smiling after me with love and joy and affection. But I didn't.

*

Paying My Bills

The wheels in my head which work out sums have always been disconnected. I have to concentrate very hard in a shop when I'm calculating my change. The shop assistants have their own method of counting money into your hand and chanting lots of figures while they do it. They recite mantras like — "And five is twenty, thirty, forty, fifty . . ." And I want to say — "Please stop counting coins and chanting things because I haven't got the faintest idea of what you are doing. Let us both retire to a little table with a pencil and paper and do a simple subtraction sum without any recitations or talking bits or stuff like that."

I feel ashamed of my mathematical dyslexia and rather than show my confusion in public I take my change and pretend to put it into my pocket. But I'm still secretly holding it in my hand so that it doesn't get mixed up with the rest of my money. Then I hide in a doorway near the shop and do the sums my own way. Sometimes I go into an office like the ESB to pay my bill and there is nobody else in the place. Years ago I would have walked straight up to the counter and done my business. Now I find myself saying to the nearest window — "Hi there ...I'll be with you in a minute." Then I head off between the coloured ropes. I'm actually walking away from the person who will be dealing with me. Then I double back on my tracks between more ropes and say — "Hi ... it's me again ... My goodness, I enjoyed that little walk. Do you have any more ropes I can stroll through before I start?"

Sometimes I pretend that I am a sheep who is going to be dipped. Ever since my days in group therapy I find myself compulsively getting into fantasies and the sheep dipping experience is one of my favourites. This is why I bleat quietly to myself when I'm standing between the ropes in banks or building societies.

Whenever you travel on the bus there is a little red hammer available for use in emergencies. I would like a similar hammer to be available on request at cash windows. You could use it whenever a coin refuses to come up off the counter. Some of them hate being lifted up. They slide around the place and frustrate your fingers. So you simply belt the counter with the hammer, the coin jumps up into the air, you shout "Hup!" and smartly catch it smartly in your pocket. The "Hup" is optional.

*

Cheques, Bills And Flowerpots

How do bills know when you've got a bit of money coming in the post? They're always doing it to me. I've just promised myself a treat, like a new pair of boots, because I'm about to be paid for a radio play. All these bills are hiding in the secret place where they congregate with their little antennae stuck up in the air. They can smell a good cheque in the next parish. Suddenly, they start to dance around in excited circles. "All right everybody! Pat's got a few bob ...Let's go and wipe him out!" My ESB bill knows exactly how much money I've got in my electricity flowerpot. I haven't got a clue how it knows but it does. No matter how many coins I stash away during the month, my bill is always for ten pounds more than I've got. So I borrow some money from my Telecom flowerpot. Even as I am removing the cash, my phone bill is hiding behind a bush in a nearby valley with its antennae twitching. "Yippee! Pat has just swiped a tenner from our flowerpot. Let's go and zap him right now!"

Cheques know when you need them badly. They live in pipelines and they live in systems. They liaise very closely with bills. Sometimes they conspire to drop through your letterbox at one and the same time. They only do this when the bills will either wipe out the cheques completely or leave you about twenty pounds short.

From time to time cheques develop a real mean streak. They don't like the colour of their ink or somebody has said something to upset them and they have to take it out on someone. This is when they deliberately give themselves indigestion and cause a hiccup in the system. Or else they swell up to twice their normal size and get stuck in the pipeline.

Really mean cheques can make certain people so ill that they can't come into the office at all. They can isolate the person who signs them with unerring accuracy and flatten them with the flu for a month. Cash was much better. Cash didn't live in pipelines and clog them up. It never got stuck in systems. People just put it into brown envelopes and gave it to you.

I was coming home from a poetry gig in Westport on the train last week. The cheque was in my pocket. I saw excited little bills peeping over stone walls at Manulla Junction. They reached my house before I did. How did they do that? How did they go faster than the train? Somebody please tell me.

*

Money For Jam

I used to love working on the fruit farms when I was a child. Everything was so simple. You filled your basket with strawberries and you handed it up. Straight away the man gave you your cash. There was no messing.   The man didn't have to initiate a cheque requisition. You didn't have to give him an invoice or a statement or anything. Nothing had to be fed into a system.

You simply handed up your strawberries and the man gave you money. It was brilliant. Getting paid used to be easy. In the days when men sat up on high stools and inscribed spidery handwriting into ledgers you always got your cash in a brown envelope when it was due and everybody was happy.

When I was a painter's assistant in a factory which manufactured bottle-washing machines, when I was a casual docker, a member of a road gang, a draught-excluder salesperson, a kitchen porter, a stand-up comic and God knows what else, I always had a healthy cash flow. Then we started to streamline things. We couldn't leave well enough alone. We rationalised and computerised and all of a sudden your cash seemed get further and further away.

For the first time in my life people on the other end of telephones started to talk to me about hiccups. A hiccup to me was always a high-pitched noise that you made when your respiratory system was temporarily up the creek. You held your breath or drank a glass of water or somebody gave you a fright and then you were all right again.

It is a dreary fact of modern life that systems which are supposed to generate cash for you are prone to multiple hiccups and there isn't a damn thing you can do about it. There is no point in creeping up behind a system unexpectedly and shouting "Boo"' because you are wasting your time.   You cannot frighten a system or give it a glass of water. It doesn't work that way.

Another equally dreary fact is that the person who signs the cheque is always away. God alone knows where they go or what they do when they get there, but they don't seem to be able to stay in the one place for more than thirty seconds at a time. I believe that when you apply for a job with a company as the person who signs the cheques they only ask you one question — "How good are you at being somewhere else all the time?" I think that I'll go back to work at the strawberries as a mature picker. At least I'll always have the price of a good dinner ...in cash ...in my pocket.

*

In The Good Old Days Sweeties Held Money

I used to feel better about the world whenever I saw it. You'd read about Conscience Money every day of the week. Someone was always paying somebody else back and little notices would appear in the paper. "M.K. acknowledges receipt of £5 conscience money." You'd read it and forget all about world wars and invasions and things like that. You'd think — "Isn't that powerful — M.K. got his fiver back."
Nobody seems to be paying him anything anymore.

Young people don't believe me when I tell them about the "Misfares" tin. If the bus conductor missed you or you forgot to pay your fare you simply put your money into the tin at the door as you were getting off. They want to know things like if you had a screwdriver in your pocket and nobody was looking, could you take the tin and all?

When you tell them about sweets which actually contained hidden money their eyes light up. Now that's more like it. Lucky Lumps which contained real cash. "Eh Pat — would the notes not be all crumpled when you got them out of your sweet?" No — there were coins in them. "Well — it must have been a huge big sweet if it had a pound coin inside it." No — when you cracked the sweet open you found a threepenny bit if you were lucky.

At that stage I was asked to work it out in real money. So I did. "Eh — if you were lucky you won the equivalent of 1.25 new pence." You can feel the ground opening up slowly under your feet as you say it. They are still looking at you and wondering what manner of person went around sucking sweets like that and putting money into tins on the bus.

I decided against telling them about the Easter Dues. I still prefer not to think about it. You sat in the church with your head down as the priest opened up the book of evidence. Then he started to read out a long list of names which started up around the five pound mark and worked its way down to pages full of widows' mites. You'd be sitting there thinking — "Please God — don't let my Da be in amongst the widows."

By the time the priest had reached the pound notes you were planning to run away from home after tea with all your marbles packed into a spotty handkerchief on the end of a stick. Then you remembered the amount that was read out earlier on — "Two pounds, ten shillings, anonymous" and you decided — "That was it, that must have been my Da." And you decided to go on living at home — at least until next Easter.

Conscience money is right.

*

Make Me a Mortgage I Can't Refuse

The word was never mentioned in school. Daddy was gone to work. Mammy was in the kitchen. Sean and Brigid were playing in the garden and the cat was on the mat. Everything was cool. But nobody ever mentioned a mortgage. I got one three years ago and the thought of it still turns my legs to jelly.

We learned a poem about an old woman of the roads. The only thing she wanted in life was a little house of her own. She dreamed about a dresser filled with shining delft. But nobody told us about interest rates. I suspect that nobody told the old woman either.   It is too late for me now. No matter how they rewrite the text books, I'm done for. I wish that I had learned, "Daddy has gone to work with a jolly song on his lips — 'Hey nonnie no, I have got a mortgage and I am the happiest daddy on this earth' ."   Mammy could have been in the kitchen going scrub-rub-a-dub and chanting: "Sean and Brigid are in the garden, the cat is on the mat and we are up-to-date with our Payments. What a merry family are we."

We never received any sex education but some things come naturally anyway. Mortgages are different. A letter was delivered by hand to my house this morning from the building society. They were inviting me to re-mortgage and take out a larger loan. I had to go upstairs and lie down for three hours in a darkened room before the banging in my head went away. The letter explained that I could build on an extension, buy a holiday home and put in double-glazing. I don't even want a dresser filled with shining delft, thank you very much. I just want the jelly in my legs to go away and annoy somebody else for a while.

We studied lots of *Aisling* poems for the Leaving Cert. The poet went off wandering through the mist and he invariably bumped into a beautiful woman who was crying her eyes out underneath a tree. She told him that she was crying because all her sons had gone away. What a perfect opportunity that was to educate us about being up to your eyes in debt. Instead of telling us that she was Mother Ireland, why didn't they explain that she was really an out-of-control mortgage? All of her sons had taken to the hills because they could spot a final demand a mile off.

At least I can relate to the old woman who lived in a shoe. That woman had her head screwed on the right way. I think if we all lived in a shoe for a while, the buzzing in our heads might stop.

*

What Do You Get When You're Fifty?

I think it's a very significant landmark in your life. So I made a start with Aras an Uachtarain. I rang them up and explained that I'll be fifty this year. Half a century. "Can you tell me how much I'll get when I hit the hundred mark?" A very friendly voice told me that I'll receive a cheque for £250 plus a personal letter from The President. "That's great but could you let me have half the money up front in August plus a nice little card or a note or something like that?" No luck. They will gladly send me out a card if I'd really like one but there's no chance of a few shillings on account.

I tried the Free Schemes next. There are some brilliant ones listed in the Green Pages. Free bottled gas, electricity, telephone rental, travel ... all sorts of fabulous stuff. God, I thought, I'll get myself some of that. The girl in Social Welfare said that I'll have to be sixty-six. "Yes — I know that but what can you do for me now to be going on with ...I'm just fifty?" The girl was very understanding. She said that she didn't make the rules and if it was left up to her I could have the lot. So I tried a bit of negotiation. "Could I have just a bit of my free electricity now please? I'll settle for the hairdryer and maybe you could throw in my vacuum cleaner while you're at it." No luck. "Well, how about a teenchy bit of my free travel, then? Down to the ILAC Library and back on the bus to change my books?" Nothing doing.

One last try. "When I'm sixty-six I know that I'll be entitled to a free licence for black and white television. I haven't got a TV so could I arrange to get the cash instead or else could I have vouchers for smoked salmon?" Forget it

Surely there's something you can get your hands on for free when you hit the fifty mark. I rang The Bank of Ireland and started again. Everybody is so nice when they're explaining that you really don't qualify for anything at all. I'm still too young for that lovely Golden Years stuff. I'm much too old for the student schemes. I'm almost fifty and stuck in the middle of nowhere. "How about starting up a Silver Years Scheme for middle-aged hippies?" The man in the bank said they'd think about it. I played my last card. "Supposing I go back to college and do a Masters Degree in Marine Biology and Oceanography? Can I get some of the free student things?" The man said we could talk about it. I'd much rather have the smoked salmon vouchers.

*

A Day In The Life

10.00 a.m. Everybody I see in town today seems to be carrying a bulging plastic bag with a new duvet in it. There are sales on everywhere, "Closing Down Sales". "Liquidation Sales". "Bankrupt Sales". We've Had it Up To Here Sales". The whole city has gone crazy.

10.30 a.m. I've joined the madness, I don't want to be the only person going home on the bus without a duvet. So I said to the man in the shop — "Could I have one of those double, 15 tog ones please?" The sign over them read "£12.99". He stuffed it into the bag and said, "£13.00 please". If there's one thing that drives me mad it's people with full-time jobs who try to rob me of my penny change. So I pointed up at the sign and demanded it. I was given my receipt and 5p change by mistake. Yippee! So perish all thriving shops who try to misappropriate my penny.

11.00 a.m. Life is great when you honestly don't care whether people think that you're mean or not. So far this morning I've picked up three twopenny pieces from shop floors, a penny off the floor of a bus and a fivepenny piece off the pavement. Added to the 4p extra that I got in the duvet shop, that comes to 16p. I think it's wonderful that so many people are shy about picking up small change. More power to their shyness.

13.00 hours. I'm standing outside the National Lottery Headquarters. The man in the G.P.O. said he couldn't pay my winnings to me because my scratch card had been bought elsewhere. Neither of us could make out the smudged name of the shop on the back. I got it as a present so I hadn't got a clue. So he sent me off to H.Q.

13.05 hours. National Lottery Headquarters is brilliant. You sink into the carpet and everything. I was hoping to be ushered into a special suite where they'd ask me to pose for pictures with a huge big cardboard cheque in my hand. Then I could drink a glass of orange and pretend that it was champagne. The girl at reception said that I couldn't have cash for security reasons so I happily settled for a cheque. It was a beauty with a lovely message typed on the back. "Dear Pat Ingoldsby, Congratulations! Please find attached cheque for your lottery win of £2.00." Two pounds ... I swear it. I once got a cheque from RTE for 85p but it wasn't nearly as nice as this one.

14.00 hours. I've picked up so much cash today that I'm taking the rest of the day off. Any money that I see on the floor of the bus can stay there because I'm resting against my 15 tog duvet. Good night and God Bless!

*

Keep In Touch And Lose Your Bank Balance

I'm always aware that every minute is costing me a fortune. I've just phoned my brother in Canada and I can picture this little digital counter clicking up the pounds like a taxi meter on fast forward. My nephew in Ontario is saying, "Hold on and I'll try to find Daddy for you — I think he's up the road somewhere." I'm pleading with him to fetch his Mammy. Now I'm talking to David. I'm asking him what time it is in Canada and what is the weather like and I'm thinking to myself, it's costing me an awful lot of money to find out. I always feel that I should be telling him important things like I've just won a million on the Lotto and I'm sending him one half. Or *Bord Fáilte* have just voted him emigrant of the year and are flying himself and the family home for an all-expenses paid holiday.

I still remember the time when I was living at home and my parents were phoning Uncle George in Atlanta. We'd all be standing around in the hall waiting for our turn to say hello.

That was all you got the chance to say because the call was costing so much. My father would whiz the receiver around and you yelled "Hello Uncle George" as fast as you could while the handset shot past your face.   Uncle George would be at the other end shouting "Who's that?" but before you had a chance to identify yourself, your brother would be yelling his "Hello Uncle George" down the phone. A transcript of the conversation would read "Hello Uncle George..."... "Who's that?" five times. I learned my long distance call technique from my parents. They also wanted to know what time it was and what the weather was like. The basic problem is that we never know whether they are having their breakfast over there or winding the alarm clock and putting the cat out. I think that the overseas operator should fill us in before we start. "Hello caller — your brother will more than likely be in his pyjamas because it's way past their bedtime over there, oh, and by the way it's lashing rain."

My brother now does the Uncle George thing to me in reverse. Young voices holler "Hello Uncle Pat," from the far side of the Atlantic Ocean while I'm seated in Dublin 3 yelling "Who's that?"

Roll on the television phone where you can see exactly who is yelling at you.

*

Torn Between Two Pillows

I was caught in the magnetic pull of the pillows. I was quite unable to help myself. There they were, in a box outside a city centre shop marked— "Two for £5". "My word," I thought. "Where would you get it?" At the same time I was telling myself — "Hang on a minute. You've got a house full of bloody pillows already. Don't go buying two more." Asthmatics tend to go overboard like that. We believe that unless we fall asleep propped up into a near standing position it is highly unlikely we will every live to see our free travel.

My father once arrived home from England with the boot of his car filled with fluffy washing-up mops. There must have been over 200 of them. It wasn't asthma in his case. "They were ten for £2.50," he explained. "You never know the day nor the hour." When my mother asked quite reasonably what we were going to do with them all my father said, "We can give them to people we like." The postman was presented with five of them that Christmas and said, "Just what I've always wanted," but the twitching muscles at the side of his face were a dead give-away. Whenever I'm in the full of my health I have no problem whatsoever with cut-price pillows. But when I'm feeling bleakly depressed they exercise a powerful hold over me. I stand there paralysed with indecision and wish that there was a crisis number which I could telephone. "For God's sake come and help me the pillows have got me again."

I know exactly what plunged me into this present depression. I firmly believe that one of my sister's cats ate my hearing aid last week and I can't afford to buy myself another one. I asked a vet yesterday if cats eat hearing aids and he said that to the best of his knowledge they don't. He couldn't swear about ostriches though. He said you could feed those lads Swiss Army knives and wristwatches and it wouldn't take a feather out of them. I'm convinced it was the cat. I was getting dressed when I spotted her munching my hearing aid on the floor. I rescued it and put it safely onto the dressing-table. Five minutes later it had vanished and the cat was wearing a distinctly ostrichey look on its face. I have been around cats most of my life and I know an ostrichey expression when I see one. It is only a matter of time before the cat begins to whistle and then I will have all the proof that I need.

*

I'd Rather Be Me

As far as I'm concerned it's over. I don't even think about it anymore. I gave up regular television work about six years ago.

It was a decision which was good for my head. You move on. You do new things.   I never felt happy with the term "celebrity". I never enjoyed being termed a "television star". I always avoided any situation which involved flashing cameras or first nights or "beautiful people". I was invited to lots of first nights and openings and closings and I preferred not to go. I find beautiful people everywhere I go.

I walked into the G.P.O. yesterday morning. Twenty or thirty excited school children suddenly recognised me. They were in Dublin on a day-trip from the West of Ireland. As far as they were concerned they had just spotted a star. As far as I was concerned I was simply me who had come in to buy a stamp. Nothing more. Nothing less. "We saw you in the Wax Museum," one boy told me, and his eyes were sparkling.

Then they all started to talk at once and lots of them had cameras and they were taking my picture. I felt very happy that they were so happy, but I also felt bewildered by the whole experience. They were relating to a period in my life which was good and fulfilling and which is now healthily over. The only time I ever think about television these days is when people tell me that I should still be doing it. I explain that I'm now finding fulfilment in other things and they invariably say — "Yeah, but how about all that money?" I have discovered that no amount of money will compensate me for doing something which doesn't feel right. That is how I broke down in the past. I would rather write good poems and live on banana sandwiches than jump up and down in front of a television camera long after the fun had gone out of it.

My poems are landing me in all sorts of trouble. People are telling me that I'm not nice anymore. After a recent Kenny Live appearance, one woman phoned in and suggested that I wash my mouth out with carbolic soap So I went home and browsed very carefully through my poetry books. I searched for a "dirty poem". That is what some people are telling me that I write. I found poems about sex. I found poems about the dignity of old age. I found erotic poems. I found poems about loneliness. I found poems about all the component parts of the human body. But I couldn't find anything dirty. Perhaps if I really put my mind to it, concentrated very hard, I could write a truly dirty poem but I honestly couldn't be bothered.

*

The Wandering Shoulder Pad

I really did try to look away. A woman adjusting her clothing is a very private affair even if she is sitting in front of you on the bus. I know that I should have kept staring out of the window but the whole business was strangely compelling. Her left shoulder-pad had slipped and wandered half-way down her sleeve. It had become lodged near her elbow and looked like one of Popeye's muscles before he swallows his spinach. She was doing her best to coax it back up her sleeve without letting anybody else know what she was doing. She wasn't finding it easy. I very much wanted to empathise with her. I wanted to tell her that sometimes when I've got a hole in the pocket of my jeans, a knobbly lump of paper hankies wanders away down my leg. It's not easy to coax a thing like that back up into your pocket in public. I wanted to tell her that sometimes my small change escapes down my leg and sets up a little money colony in my boot. It is deeply embarrassing at the supermarket checkout when you finish up with one boot on and one boot off because you need to get at the fifty pence piece which is under your sock. More than anything I wanted to help the poor woman but you don't know what to say. You can't tip a complete stranger on the back and murmur, "Excuse me, Madam — I couldn't help noticing that your left shoulder pad is wedged down near your elbow. Kindly permit me to work it back up to the top of your sleeve for you." We haven't yet manufactured a euphemism for slipped shoulder pads. A man recently informed me that I had got cheese on my chin and I knew exactly what he was talking about. Offence was neither

given nor taken. But we haven't yet come up with a sensitive way of saying, "Your pad is down near your elbow." Perhaps we could whisper gently, "There is yoghurt half-way down your arm." This is something we need to work on.   When the unfortunate woman did succeed in returning the pad to its rightful place, her problems were only beginning. It was now sticking up in a side-ways position like the kingpole in a circus tent. Every time she hammered it down flat with her fist the thing just popped up again. Her left shoulder was now approximately six inches taller than her right. My nerves were in bits. One good decisive thump and I could have flattened it for her but I was afraid that the driver would put me off the bus. There is a very strong case to be made for either Bluetack or Superglue.
*

Pishes, Yups And Whees

I nearly die of fright every time it happens. All of a sudden, and without any warning, a bus lets out a terrifying 'PISSSSSHHHHH!' My heart starts to pound and I get funny little tingling pains in the tips of my fingers. I don't think that buses should be allowed to 'PISH' at people like that.   I don't mind whales 'PISHING'. They are out in the middle of the ocean where they are not going to put the heart across anybody. Every so often they have to let out a huge big gush of water and more power to their spouts. If somebody was going past in a rowing boat I think that whales would have the decency to hold onto their gush for a couple of seconds.

I think that it has got something to do with air brakes. Every so often a bus feels the need to do a mighty 'PISH'. That is all very well but some of us have got weak hearts and hypertension. A really unexpected 'PISH' could give you a cardiac arrest and then where would you be?   I think that buses should let out a little warning 'Bip bip bip' first. Or failing that there should be a special reserved area in the city centre where they can park and 'PISH' away to their hearts' content.

When the Yupping Man disappeared from the streets of Dublin all the tingling pains in my fingers vanished too. He used to wander around the city centre shouting 'YUP' at people. There was a wild glory in some of his 'YUPS' which could send your whole past life flashing in front of your eyes.

I remember being discharged from Baggot Street Hospital after two weeks of oxygen, drips and injections. I was feeling very vulnerable. Buses didn't 'PISH' at you in those days. But Your-Man sprang out of a chemist's doorway and unleashed a resounding 'YUP' which almost put me straight back into intensive care.   He's gone now but there are far worse things than 'YUPS'. Sometimes I'm walking past a parked car and without a word of warning it starts to go 'WHEE WHEE WHEE' at me.

I haven't been attempting to pick its lock or stuff a potato up the exhaust pipe or anything. Straight away I feel like taking a stand. Part of me wants to confront the car and say "Now listen pal - don't you start 'WHEE WHEEING' at me or I'll have your hubcaps for garters!"   I feel like standing up to buses the same way, "One more 'PISH' out of you and I'll tie a knot in your windscreen wipers."   What with 'PISHES' and 'WHEES' and Spanish students it's going to be a long hot summer.

*

Next Time I'll Hitch

19.30 p.m.— It is now one hour since the coach left Galway for Dublin. I have already suffered damage to my nervous system from which it may never recover. A non-stop barrage of jerky, abrasive, pop music is exploding out of the little black speakers in the walls of the bus and is invading my body. Repetitious rap music which is drilling in through my ears and feels like it is trying to take out my tonsils. I think it has also reached my pancreas and aorta and they are retreating down through my legs.

19.45 p.m.— I can't swear to it but I think there are now tears coming out of my ears. The music seems to have hunted my appendix up behind my forehead and now my ears have started to cry. My spirit is completely broken. If somebody will stop the rapping I am prepared to confess to starting The Hundred Years War, take full responsibility for the beheading of Anne Boleyn and admit to masterminding the sacking of Drogheda.

19.50 p.m.— Now I want to do a wee wee as well. But let there be no panic. The guy in front of me has just been up to speak to the driver and now he is heading down towards the back of the bus. Saints be praised. There is a toilet on board. I'll just play it cool and let the guy return to his seat. Then I'll wait for ten minutes or so and saunter casually down to the back.

20.00 p.m.— You go down a steep set of steps at the back and there are two doors. One is marked 'Emergency Exit' so you don't open that one. But there is no handle on the toilet door and it is resolutely shut. I'm trying to force my fingers in behind it and I'm putting my thumb in through a hole where the handle should be. Then I suddenly thought . . . supposing there is somebody in there and here I am attempting to force the door open. They might take fright and bite my thumb off and you couldn't honestly blame them.

20.05 p.m.— A young man is telling me that the toilet is, in fact, empty but you need an official key to get in and the key is held by the driver. So I swayed up the aisle to the front and asked him why in heaven's name do you need a key to do a wee-wee. "So that lots of people won't use the toilet," he said.

20.10 p.m.— The key is singularly appropriate. It is like an exact replica of the T-shaped one used by Water Board officials to turn off the supply at the mains. Once inside the toilet you had to keep all your wits about you and allow for constant changes of direction. I have done more relaxed wee-wees on trawlers in the Hebrides during force six gales.

20.15 p.m.— The driver agreed to switch off the music between Tyrellspass and Dublin. I felt like giving him all my money and the title deeds to my house.

*

The Call Of The Concrete

13.15 hours. The wet concrete seemed to be daring me. Lovely virgin concrete beside the bus stop. Smooth and wet without a mark or a blemish. "Go on, Pat, I dare you. Write your name in me." There was nobody else at the bus-stop. No witnesses. My heart began to pound.

13.17 hours. I was always very good as a little boy. The very worst I ever did was knock on a door and run away. Once was really daring and wrote with chalk on the path: "P.I. XX A.H." I wrote it right outside her front gate. Then she broke my heart by writing "A.H. XX B.R." beside it. I never liked B.R. very much but I really couldn't stand him after that.

13.20 hours. Still no sign of the bus. Perhaps I should bend down very casually and pretend to be tying my shoelace. Then I can write "Pat" very quickly before anybody comes.

13.25 hours. Where did the old lady come from? She's sure to tell somebody on me. Perhaps I can get her involved in some way. Then she'll be an accomplice. That's it. I'll ask her to keep nix and if anybody comes along while I'm doing it she can create a diversion by setting fire to her buggy.

13.27 hours. "That's a lovely day now," I said. She smiled and said "Thank God." Then I sounded her out. "It's a lovely day for writing your name in wet concrete." To my astonishment she looked down at the concrete, looked up at me and said "As long as you don't get caught."

13.29 hours. She advised me to disguise my handwriting because that way the Corporation couldn't get samples of it and confront me in court with plaster casts and photographs. I'd swear that she'd done it before. She even covered me with her buggy while I bent down and traced my name with a trembling finger. It's an incredible feeling. You get completely carried away. You feel like whipping off your shoes and socks and plonking your feet into the concrete as well.

13.32 hours. I was tempted to stand guard and miss successive buses and only leave when the concrete had set. The old lady advised me that behaviour like that would be a complete give-away. She said that whenever she wants to get a really good buzz, she goes down to the supermarket and whams her coffee jars into the bottle bank.

13.35 hours. We sat together on the bus. She said that her late husband once wrote their two names in the sand on Malahide strand and drew a heart around them with a stick. Then they both sat there and watched as the tide came in and washed their names away.

13.36 hours. She whispered her initials into my ear and winked at me. It shall be done.

*

Making A Show Of You

I feel mortified when it happens. I insert my bus ticket into the automatic checker and the machine suddenly goes crazy. Everyone else gets a nice little beep . . . a beep which says, "This good law-abiding person has got an honest-to-God, up-to-date ticket. Our country needs more people like this."

I get a high-speed series of electronic insults which tell the whole bus "Do you see this guy? He's a millionaire who doesn't need to travel like an ordinary person yet here he is trying to do Dublin Bus with a dodgy ticket. Hanging is too good for him."

It's too late when the driver says, "Don't worry about it. That machine has been acting up all day." He doesn't announce it over his microphone. He tells you in a quiet voice which nobody else hears. The damage is done.

It's exactly the same feeling as when the bishop decides to stop beside you in the church on your Confirmation morning and ask you all sorts of questions about your school. He spends ages asking you things and you wish that he'd pick on somebody else because the whole church thinks you're missing your catechism question and making a show of your parents.

You want to ask the bishop to straighten his mitre and announce in a loud voice, "This inspired young Christian has correctly told me that there are three divine persons in one God. He's simply telling me now that the strawberry jam in his lunch sandwiches leaks out all over his copybooks and that's perfectly cool as far as I'm concerned." But bishops don't make announcements like that.

I remember a huge crowd kneeling outside the confession box. I wasn't unduly worried because I'd only told three lies and been disobedient twice. It was a simple in and out, say Three Hail Marys job. I'd only got as far as my first lie when the priest discovered that he'd met an uncle of mine on the foreign missions.

He wanted to know all sorts of detailed medical stuff like whether Uncle Michael's sinuses were still blocked up first thing in the morning. All I wanted to do was sort out my two disobedients and get out of there as fast as I could but this man was really into blocked sinuses in a big way

I was praying for an announcement to flash up over the door outside 'This penitent is merely discussing the early morning state of his uncle's nostrils.' Perhaps they have signs like that now. I don't really know. It's been ten years, nine months. six weeks, five days and counting since my last confession
*

Still A Long Way To Listowel

Six hours on a bus is an awful long time. Dublin to Listowel. Parental voices began to haunt me in Busaras. "You should have gone before we left Dublin." So I did. Three wee-wees in twenty minutes. Then I took my place in the queue.

I was quietly repeating a mantra over and over again in my head. "I will not want to go again between here and Listowel." I made my first tactical error on boarding the bus. I checked to see if there was a toilet on board. Panic. Blind unreasoning panic. Ahhhhh! How could Bus Eireann do a thing like this to me. I am undone.

The bus pulled out of Busaras at half past one. I was trying to calm myself. Perhaps the driver suffers from weak kidneys. Perhaps he'll have to stop at every single pub on the way and race inside. In that case I won't be very far behind him. I checked his face in the driving mirror. No such luck. The man is utterly relaxed and carefree.

Ten minutes down-range and I was still OK This is crazy. If I keep monitoring myself like this I'll be bursting before we get to the Naas Road. Think of something else. Anything at all. *Dominus vobiscum. Et cum spirit tu tuo.* I went through as much of the altar-boy Latin as I could remember. That got me as far as Newbridge.

Oh no. Here comes The Curragh. All those bushes. Try not to look at them. Talk to the person beside you. "Hello-my name is Pat and I do not want to do a wee-wee." You can't say anything like that. I wonder how everyone else on the bus is getting on. How many of them are sitting there thinking about altar-boy Latin.

I really should have gone by train. I can manage Heuston to Cork on just the one tinkle. That is a very impressive average. Mind you, that is only if I am sitting in an outside seat. If I am trapped on the inside I'm in deep trouble before the train gets out of Dublin county.

It's exactly the same in the cinema. Sit me at the end of a row and I can outlast the best of them. Put me in the centre and I'm gone before they tell you about the fire exits.

I shall never know how I managed to hold out from Portlaoise to Roscrea. It was murder. A judicious blend of knotting my legs, inspired self-control and thinking about *Italian for Beginners*. When the driver announced a 15-minute halt there was a beautifully restrained stampede. Nobody actually broke into a gallop, yet the bus was empty before he applied the hand brake. Nobody drank more than one coffee. It was still a long way to Listowel.
*

Bitter bus battle over blocking buggy

The old woman left her buggy in everybody's way on the bus. She wedged it squarely in the middle of the aisle. Then she sat on the edge of her seat and hung onto it. The bus was still parked at the terminus.   An old man got on and stared at the buggy. Then he stared hard at the old woman. He spoke to her in a very loud voice as he squeezed past it. "How the hell do you expect people to get past with that thing in the way!?" "Well, you're managing OK. aren't you?" she replied in an even louder one. I don't think he should have referred to her buggy as "that thing". It had the same effect on her as when somebody kicks Clint Eastwood's mule in the "Dollar" films. Nothing short of ten inspectors would make her move it now.   While they were still saying things to each other in loud voices, a young woman got up and tried to shift it out of the way. The buggy must have been filled with pre-cast concrete blocks or something. Not only could she not budge it, but she found herself caught in a very dangerous crossfire.   Another old man got on. The bus was moving on. He clung onto the bars and glowered at the buggy. Then he made a very angry announcement. "That thing is in my way"' I felt sorry for the old woman. Everybody was giving out to her and calling her beloved buggy a "thing". If I'd been her, I would have been apologising at this stage and begging for forgiveness. But she was in towering form. She simply folded her arms and kept saying very loud defiant things.   The old man was determined not to pass the buggy and just stood there hanging on for dear life. He was jerking this way and that with the motion of the bus. Now two or three more old people were giving out hell to each other. I couldn't help wondering where all these cranky senior citizens were coming from. Usually they talked to each other about what a grand day it is, thank God. Now they're all yelling about a buggy.

One old man stood up to get off the bus. He stood up and started to kick the buggy. I swear it. His eyes were flashing and he began to boot it as hard as he could. I didn't know where to be looking. The old woman shouted, "Don't you kick my buggy that thing cost me £30." The pressure was clearly getting to her because now she was calling the buggy "thing" as well. The old man gave the buggy a parting kick and got off at the next stop. Thanks be to God their grandchildren weren't there to see it.

*

When Car Ownership Doesn't Uplift You

Some people prefer to drive to work on their own. They don't like giving lifts. This must get very tricky at times because there are often a couple of bus stops near your home. You have to get past them without seeing anybody you know. Only then are you in the clear. Some drivers use the rigid neck and stare fixedly straight ahead. They actually know who they are not seeing. They have checked while they're still downwind. "Oh no there's your-man. If he catches me, I'm gone." When they get safely past the queue, they check in the mirror. What they dread seeing is two or three people pointing after the car and giving out hell to each other. Once the game is up you very often have to change your route.

Some drivers will actually stop if they realise they they've been spotted. "God—I nearly didn't see YOU there, I was gone past the-queue before I realised it was YOU." They will definitely change their route next time out. What some of these drivers don't realise is that very often the whole thing works in reverse.

Somebody in the queue spots them in the distance and dives in behind a newspaper. "Oh no, look who's coming. Please God don't let them see me."

It is very hard to say no when somebody offers you a lift. It's even harder when they start moving piles of paper and briefcases off the front seat. "Hop in. I'm not actually going there but I'll drop you off as near as makes no difference." If you are not very careful, you are going to finish up miles out of your way. You can very easily find yourself in the middle of nowhere wondering, "How the hell did I get here?"

Sometimes they are going exactly where you wish to go. "Hop in, it's no trouble. I just have a few little things to take care of on the way." It would only seem ungrateful to say: "Thanks all the same but I'll get the bus." So you get in. Thirty minutes later, you have been in and out of a car-wash, picked up two parcels, dropped off six packages and visited a Pass machine. If you had walked you'd have been there ten minutes ago.

 Sometimes a well-meaning car stops down-range from the bus queue, the door opens and the driver starts to beep his horn. Nobody knows who he is beeping at. Nobody wants to risk rejection so everybody stands there looking at one another. Whoever does get the lift knows that the rest of the queue is going to hate them anyway. Sometimes you're better off walking.

*

I Am Not A Car Person

I can't tell one car from another. They all look exactly the same to me. Manufacturers spend millions in an attempt to invade my subconscious. They drop their cars from tall cranes, wham them over dizzy cliffs and hire nubile women to lather them with soap suds. Cranes sometimes look different to me. I can even spot the differences between dizzy cliffs. But the cars and the women all look like they have come out of the same mould.

I can still tell a VW Beetle a mile off. That was my father's very first car. He bought it in the days when there was no such thing as a driving test. You simply asked a neighbour how to start and stop the thing and you hit the open road. You worked out all the other stuff as you went along. I can still recognise a Morris Minor because Mr O'Hara bought one of those. He dropped down to ask my father about starting and stopping because my dad had two weeks experience by that stage. Then they both wandered up to ask Mr Sheridan about how to put it into reverse because he had been seen travelling backwards.

Every make of car seemed to have a different shape. Indicators flipped out of the side like little yellow fingers. Running boards were carpeted with black rubber. Mr Ryan even used a starting handle. Word spread like wildfire whenever he came out of his house. "Quick lads, in behind the hedge. Here comes Mr Ryan with his starting handle." We used to crouch down in absolute silence and watch him rolling up his sleeves. One laugh and you were dead. After the first couple of jerks with the handle, he would stop and glare at his car with malevolent hatred. After the next few attempts, he used to attack it with his right foot. Sometimes he shouted things while he was kicking it. He never seemed to worry about denting the bodywork or bruising his foot. Mr Ryan always kicked a Ford Anglia.

If I ever do get a car, I want one with a personalised design to it. I would like a double-decker model with an anchor for throwing out if I can't stop it. The upper saloon is for bringing my cats down to see the vet. I don't want them travelling downstairs and leaping on my shoulders while I'm trying to drive. Apart from that, I'm fairly easy.

*

On The Bus

I always like to allow a decent cooling-down period. The seat on the bus is still warm when somebody stands up. I most certainly do not wish to sit down on the warmth of a total stranger's bottom. It upsets my equilibrium.

I fully realise that it won't harm me. It's not like nuclear radiation or anything like that. But I still like to wait. Unfortunately other people are not so fussy. They will swipe the seat before it is decently cold. I wish that it was possible to place a 'Reserved' sign on it. A sign which reads — "I bags this seat but do not wish to sit on it while it radiates body temperature, so hands off."

I don't like sitting on an outside seat very much especially when a woman with shopping bags is sitting on the inside. Every so often she arranges her bags and grips the handles and I tense myself. Any second now. Get ready. This woman is obviously preparing to get off the bus. Then she lets go of the bags again and relaxes back into her seat and so do I. A couple of seconds later she is at it again and I'm getting all tensed up for a second time and I feel like saying — "Will you for God's sake make up your mind." Little things like that can play havoc with your head.

I don't wish to read other peoples' letters on the bus. I have said this to my eyes time and time again. "Now listen eyes — if somebody beside me takes out a letter and begins to read it I don't want either of you to start squinting sideways." But they never listen.

It's even worse if the person beside me takes out a wallet of colour photos of a party in someone's house. They are flicking through pictures of half-clad bodies on sofas and men in their underpants holding pints of beer. I'm doing my level best to look straight ahead but my eyes keep forcing themselves sideways. I try to close them but my eyelids are part of the conspiracy as well and they refuse to shut.

Sometimes I stand up when I see an old person getting onto a crowded bus and I offer them my seat. And they reject me. I feel terrible. It's even worse when someone else stands up seconds later and the old person accepts their offer. I sit there wondering — "My God — what is wrong with me?" I heard a woman yesterday telling a bus driver where he wasn't going. She looked into the bus and said — "You're not going to Sutton ..." She was absolutely right.

*

Is That What You Really Said?

It's not so bad at the main-line station. If people come down to see you off they can't get past the ticket barrier. You are spared the scene where you are sitting in your seat and they are standing in a little group outside your window. You've said everything that has to be said but the bloody train is still motionless in the station.

You wish they would go away. They wish that the train would start. Suddenly they feel the need to tell you all sorts of things. If they were crucial messages about life and death matters you wouldn't mind. When people mouth words at you through windows with urgent expressions you expect to be told something worthwhile like — "That man beside you has got sticks of gelignite taped around his stomach." You concentrate very hard while the people on the platform look as if they are reading the news for the very deaf. Their mouths are moving with big exaggerated words and you expect to receive life-saving intelligence like — "The driver of this train fully intends to take it up to about 300 mph outside Portarlington." When you finally break down the message it is something like, "Don't forget to tell Mammy that the chicken Kiev was lovely ."

When people are telling you things through the glass it is very important to look as if you understand every word they are mouthing. Otherwise they will switch over to animated mime. This is far worse. Suddenly they are waggling fingers at you and making shapes in the air with their hands and you want to slide in under the table and pretend you've never seen any of them in your life.

I've never seen 'Play the Game', but a lot of people have. If one of them is sitting beside you in the carriage they are going to figure out the messages before you do. I don't like the idea of a total stranger telling me — "She says she still loves you in spite of the other things."

I have seen extremely trendy young adults mortified by their mammies who wreck their laid-back image with messages like -"Don't forget to say your prayers ...I've packed you some good warm woolly underthings - make sure you wear them and don't go getting into bad company".

The last minute message is the one that utterly unnerves me. The one where they race alongside the train and don't stop signalling wildly to you until they have run out of platform. That's the one you worry about.

*

On The Railway

YOU shouldn't tell children things unless you really mean them. I still feel bad about the steam engine I was promised in 1949. I've got witnesses and everything. The station-master at Raheny said that he'd give me a real steam engine if I got all my sums right. My two brothers were there. They heard him.

I got all my bloody sums right. Every single one of them. But the station-master never came through with his side of the bargain. He said that they were clean out of steam engines in the stores. My father bought me a bag of bullseyes to soften the blow but there is a very significant difference between a quarter pound of sweets and a great big thundering locomotive.

I honestly never realised that the hurt was still buried deep down in my subconscious. I have been through all sorts of intensive psychotherapy during my dark days. Psychologists showed me coloured blobs which reminded me of unicorns, edible confession boxes and three-headed Popes. But even under deep hypnosis I never once mentioned steam engines.

Last week I brought home a long-playing record called "Sounds Of The Steam Age" I had been feeling very anxious recently and I thought it might help me to relax. The beginning of Side One seriously unnerved my three cats. They were already partially freaked by the sight of their owner lying down in a darkened room clutching a green flag.

Suddenly the room was filled with the sound of bleating sheep and vibrant birdsong. My cats quite reasonably assumed that the house was now full of phantom sheep and invisible blackbirds They hid upstairs behind the immersion and I don't honestly blame them. That was when an express train hissed and steamed from one speaker to another and I suddenly heard a voice which I recognised as my own demanding the locomotive which I was promised in 1949. "I want my steam engine and I want it now ...I don't want bons bons or bullseyes ... I want my steam engine."

It's not fair. That station-master was working for Great Northern Railways. He made me a promise while acting as their agent. I have no intention of being unreasonable. I'm not going to take legal action against Iarnrod Eireann because it's not their fault. They probably haven't got any spare steam engines anyway. But I want one. I got my sums right. If there is any decency and fair play left in this world I will get one. Perhaps I have never really suffered from endogenous depression at all. Maybe if that man had kept his promise in 1949 there would never have been a bother on me.
*

The wind would skin you on Platforms 6 and 7 at Connolly Station. It's a bleak and desolate place and you stand there with your feet numb and your eyes watering.

A man with tears in his eyes said, "Wouldn't you think all the same they'd put empty oil barrels with holes in them along the platform. Then you could light fires and huddle around them singing warm songs and roasting chestnuts."

"You could roast potatoes as well and boil some water for tea," said a woman who was giving out hell about the cardboard cups they give you with your coffee. "They have these thin flimsy handles," she said. "And the coffee tips all over you. By the time it has soaked through your clothes, it's all cold and it freezes to your body."

A pigeon landed on the platform and the cold wind hit him. He stuck his head in underneath his wing and said he was never taking it out again. Another pigeon landed on the railway tracks and started to walk the line towards Rosslare. I think it's warmer down there because of the Gulf Stream.

One very old man swore that when he was very young he used to stand on these same platforms. "Once I remember that the Czar of Russia's private train came hurtling through here on its way to St. Petersburg or Omsk or somewhere. And there was a blizzard swirling around it and timber wolves chasing along in its wake. We were all huddled together singing hymns and we tried to wave to the Czar but our arms were that brittle with the cold that they fell off and broke on the platform."

"You sometimes get that," said another man who was sitting down all the time because he was frozen to a bench and couldn't get up until a paramedic came along and freed him with a blowlamp.

One woman said "Hang on a minute." She was addressing the old man who had seen the timber wolves. "If your arms fell off with the cold how come you still have them?"

"They grew again," he said. "It was during Queen Victoria's reign d'ye see. Things were a lot better than."

A DART pulled in with 'Bray' written on the front. A lot of people got onto it even though they wished to travel in the Howth direction. They said that they wanted to go somewhere before their bodies went rigid. There were already some Bray people on board who had travelled out to Howth for the same reason. They had now regained the use of their limbs. Limerick Junction isn't great either.

*

SOME people go through life convinced that they are going to get onto the wrong train. They buy a ticket to Cork. And they are directed towards platform 2. A sudden panic attack grips them en route. "Supposing the man in the ticket office thought that I really meant Galway. Oh my God ... I'd better ask somebody."   So they ask a porter. And they always ask the question as if they are doing it for the very first time. He points towards Gate 2. There is a very large sign over it which says "Queue here for Cork." So they walk over and stand beside the gate.   That is when the conspiracy theory takes over. "My God . . . supposing the whole thing is really an Iarnrod Eireann conspiracy to get me onto the Waterford train. I'd better ask somebody." So they ask the person beside them. "Eh-are you going to Cork?" The person shakes his head. "No-I'm only going as far as Limerick Junction." This compounds the panic. Railway tracks go off in different directions at junctions. Supposing some of the carriages go one way and some of them go another. I'd better ask somebody.   So they ask a man in a very smart uniform with braid on his cap: the stationmaster. He is bound to know. "Excuse me ... does every carriage on this train go to Cork? I mean — do I have to sit at the back or the front or in a specially numbered carriage or anything?" "No. This is the Cork train in its entirety. Every single bit of it. Don't worry. You're at the right gate. Just wait here. Everything is grand." So they wait. And they look at their ticket. All sorts of numbers on it. And the fare. And the date. But wait a minute. It doesn't mention Cork. In fact it doesn't mention anywhere. I'd better ask somebody.   It now becomes crucial that they get a definite categorical answer from the ticket checker at the gate.   "Is this the right train for Cork?" He points at it. "That's it . . . that's the one." At this stage they wouldn't be reassured if every single carriage had the word 'Cork' emblazoned on the side in six-foot high luminous flashing letters. But they get onto it anyway because they can still ask the person beside them, the person

who comes around selling cups of coffee and the man on board who clips your ticket.
We need people like this because they are actually asking the question for us.
*

On The Road Again

I hadn't hitched since Jimi Hendrix played at Woodstock. Wandering down towards Spain with your thumb sticking out trying to find yourself. I'd completely forgotten what it was like. I arrived at Galway railway station last week to catch the 8.45 am bus to Clifden. I was three weeks too late. They were now into the winter schedule and there was no bus until the afternoon. I was due on stage in the Community School at 12 noon. I was standing beside a sign which said 76 kilometres to Clifden. I arranged my face into a nice friendly unthreatening expression and stuck my thumb out. Almost everybody who was driving in the opposite direction recognised me. They waved and grinned. "My God-if only you were going into Galway we'd love to give you a lift." A lot of drivers who were heading out of Galway waved and smiled. "If only we weren't turning off at the next corner we'd take you all the way." Fair enough.
   Three cars stopped almost immediately. Suddenly the three teenage girls further down the road were gone. I tried very hard to psyche myself into a fantasy where I looked like a teenage girl. It used to work in group therapy but I hadn't got a grey moustache then.
   A man called Michael gave me a lift to Moycullen. It was filled with early morning mist and birdsong and three women who kept looking over at me and talking to one another. The air was tinged with Autumn and watery sun and I would love to have stayed there and nourished my spirit. A man called John gave me a lift in his lorry. I was perched high up in his bumpy cab looking out at black trees and still lakes and mountains with

immense white clouds resting up against them. Myself and John looked at the sky reflected in water, and the trees bent over by the wind and his cab was full of the easy silence when you don't need to be saying anything.

Now I was standing beside mounds of cut turf. A narrow road. One bird was singing but I couldn't see it. The only other sound was a stream splashing. No people. Nature held me and it was good. After a long time a car came.

Maureen dropped me right outside the Community School in Clifden. I felt curiously different. A part of me, which had been dead for a long time, was breathing again. Nature touched me.
*

At The Airport

I love attaching myself onto the end of a queue at the airport. You have to be doing something when you're hanging around waiting for a friend off a flight. I especially love to join a queue of people who are checking in for a really long flight to New York or Adelaide or somewhere like that.

Everybody shuffles forward with suitcases and hold-alls. And I shuffle with them. Muscles are twitching at the side of people's faces. Some of them have got very white knuckles. I even twitch a few muscles of my own just to enter into the spirit of the thing. Then when I reach the check-in desk, I veer away and feel an intense glow of relief. A sort of "Phew, that was close" feeling. It's lovely.

I like to stand near a group of women who are waiting for an incoming long-distance flight. The chances are they're going to meet a sister or a brother they haven't seen for years. As soon as the person arrives, there are going to be hugs and embraces flying all over the place.   It's best to loiter at the edge of the group and wait for the outburst of tears and hugs. Then you flit in and out saying things like, "Hello, I'm Joe's eldest." Or "Great to see you - I'm Martin's second youngest." People will grab you and kiss you and hold you, and before you know where you are, there'll be tears coursing down your cheeks as well. Try not to get too involved or you could very well finish up in somebody's car speeding towards Donegal or Bandon. Nobody ever asks pilots or air hostesses questions. They seem to be overawed by the uniform. Sometimes I give them my address and ask them not to be flying their planes over my house. I find them very good about things like that. They're only waiting to be asked.

*

Cats, Beetles And Granny's Toenails

I've never seen anything like it. The archaeologist on my mother's television could hardly speak with the excitement. His eyes were sparkling. "We have just discovered nine tons of mummified cats." He wasn't joking. He said that the ancient Egyptian hillside behind him contained a rare treasure trove of embalmed pussy cats.

I have no idea how he weighed them. I would dearly love to know what he intends to do with them. Perhaps on the ninth day of Christmas he plans to give his true love nine tons of mummified cats. I don't really know.

In about one thousand years time from now they'll be digging up things which we have buried. I have decided to be cremated because I don't wish to cause the archaeologists of the future any confusion. During an operation on my stomach some years ago the surgeon put some plastic into my tummy. He said that I've got a congenital weakness there and the plastic will help to keep all my spare parts in place.

I don't want some poor guy to dig me up one thousand years from now and decide after he analyses the contents of my stomach that in the year 1990 we all ate lumps of plastic. They can do without that sort of disinformation.

Cats were treated like gods in ancient Egypt. Me and my brother used to treat beetles the same way when were little. We used to snuggle them up in matchboxes full of cotton wool when they died. Then we said Mass over them and buried them in the back garden.

In one thousand years from now some wildly excited archaeologist will be standing where our back garden used to be. He'll be freaking out into a television camera. "We have just uncovered a rich twentieth century burial ground for sacred beetles." I don't think we buried nine tons of them but we planted more than enough to excite the average archaeologist. My granny used to bury her toenails. She believed that on the last day they will all rise up again glorious and immortal for the Last Judgement.

We used to tell her that Almighty God will be so busy with crowd control He won't have time to be pronouncing judgement on her twentieth century toenails. But her faith was unshakeable. I hope that they will remain undisturbed until the final trumpet blows. I shudder to think what conclusions might be drawn on them in one thousand years time. Sacred beetles and edible plastic are bad enough without that kind of thing.
*

The Case For The Cobweb

My conscience starts to nag me as soon as I reach for the sweeping brush. "How could you? That little spider spent hours building his web. He's not doing you any harm." "Yeah, well he should go and build it somewhere else. I mean, right outside my front door is a bit much. That cobweb is probably bringing down my property value." Then I go out with the brush and stand there for a while.

I have to give him this much. His cobweb is a miracle of ageless engineering. He spins perfect symmetry all around him. He doesn't have any plans or anything. He just seems to carry all the calculations around with him in his head. "Go on then. Do it. Go on, you home wrecker. You're worse than those Victorian landlords who used to evict expectant mothers into blizzards." "Come on-it's only a cobweb. That little guy can spin miles of the stuff any time he feels it. Besides, I'm really doing him a favour. Every time it rains here he gets soaked."

I wouldn't mind so much if he did his housework. I think that I could live with a lovely pristine silver web. Decent God-fearing spiders get rid of things like fluff and leaves. This little guy is lazy as sin. He couldn't care less.   I finally did it. I closed my eyes, swished the brush and away went the spider, cobweb and all. "I hope you're proud of yourself. With one swipe of your brush, you have effectively undermined the balance of nature." I felt awful.

One hour later he was hard at it again. If I was a parish priest, I'd write a sermon about him. His whole world is blitzed by a marauding brush and he doesn't race off to moan to his mother. He is too busy spinning and measuring up all over again.

Auctioneers don't help. Their windows are full of coloured photographs of houses for sale. But they never include the cobwebs.   Glossy magazines are worse. They are always showing us the interiors of famous peoples' homes. You never see the cobwebs. It's no wonder that so many of us reach for the sweeping brush.   But not any more. I'm putting a preservation order on that cobweb. If you wish to buy my house, you have to sign a solemn declaration not to interfere with it Otherwise it's no deal.

*

A Word In Your Ear About Fleas

A friend of mine called round last night. We were sitting in the house and every so often a little black object pinged up in the air out of the carpet. I knew exactly what it was. After a while there were three of them. Pinging up and down.

He must have noticed but he was very polite. He could have said, "No offence but there are live objects leaping up into the air as we speak." But he didn't. We just sat there and talked. Perhaps he went home afterwards and told his wife that my house is hopping. I hope not.

I think that they are exhibitionist fleas who aren't happy unless they're making a show of me. I can sit all day long by myself in the house and nothing stirs. Perhaps they're resting. As soon as a visitor crosses my threshold, I think that they all whisper to one another. "Hey, we've got company. I bags the first jump."

I don't hold it against my cats. I know that they don't do it on purpose. They don't want little hoppers any more than I do. I'm quite certain that they don't go out at night and have competitions to see who can bring home the most.

I bought a huge packet of special powder and rambled around the house like a biblical farmer scattering seeds over his land. When the white stuff settled into the carpet, there was a dramatic pause which you could almost hear.

All of a sudden they started to jump so high that I though they would never come down again. I don't know what is in the powder but I suspect that it's some sort of speed. Little black yokes whizzed up into the air. They did vertical take-offs and backward flips that put me in mind of Mexican jumping beans. I prayed to God that nobody would ring the doorbell.

When we were kids, there was only ever the one. We had three cats but there was only ever the one flea. We used to search the sheets and blankets with all the excitement of a Bengal tiger hunt. When it was captured we all cheered and hugged one another.

I've got millions of them. It may well have started with just one but he didn't waste any time in putting the word out. "Get round here fast boys. This is a brilliant house. Your man puts powder into the carpets which helps you to triple your jump. You won't know yourself after a week."

I'll say this much for them. They haven't actually jumped on top of anybody yet. I will take it very personally if they ever do.

*

When Did You Last See One?

If I hadn't washed my kitchen floor I would never have found out about 109 million pigs. I was putting newspapers down to cover my floor until it was dry. Next thing I was sitting on the wet floor quite unable to speak. "The EEC pig population currently stands at 109 million." That is what I read. I opened my mouth and attempted to say "my goodness" but no words came out. There are enough pigs there to fill every single soccer stadium in Europe. You could probably fill all the cinemas with pigs as well and still have lots left over. I'm sure that's not even the exact figure. I'm sure they did their pig census and then rounded it up to the nearest million. That's probably the way that you count them.

Where are they all? I have questioned students who were all over Europe during the summer and they never even saw one. Where do they keep them? Why aren't they all out in the fields snuffling and snouting and having the time of their lives rolling around in the muck? That is what pigs do. The last time I saw a pig in Ireland was in 1983. I was doing a live radio broadcast from a pig pen in Pet's Corner at Dublin Zoo until the pig munched through my microphone cable and put me off the air. I certainly didn't hold it against him. If he had been standing in my kitchen telling the whole nation about the way that I live I would probably have chewed up his cable as well.

During the last month I've been criss-crossing this island on buses and trains and haven't seen one pig. I have thrust my head out of train windows and listened very closely. I want to be able to address a carriage full of fellow travellers and say "Hark and hist! Let us glory to the sound of that ecstatic grunting!" So far my quest has been fruitless.

According to the newspaper on my kitchen floor there are 1.4 million porkers in the 26 counties. Mind you, the date on the paper was the 27th of April last so God knows how many more little piglets have been born since then. I call upon our pig breeders to let them out. We've got fields full of cows and sheep and horses. What are you afraid of? Do you think that the pigs would all climb up trees and fall out or what? Perhaps RTE Television could show us a different pig every night at closedown and tell us its first name. I'd go to bed happy after that.

*

Binbags, Bottles And Prawns

I couldn't bear to watch. The binmen were heaving big plastic bags full of rubbish into the back of the lorry. Huge metal teeth were coming down and grinding the poor defenceless bags into a pulp. In my mind I could hear them shrieking "Eeeek!" and "Arrgh!" Part of me wanted to plead for mercy. "Aw, come on, lads-that's a terrible thing to be doing to trusting bin-bags." But then I remembered how the man in the pub reacted when I spoke up on behalf of the whiskey bottles.

I couldn't take my eyes off them. Whiskey, vodka and gin bottles all suspended upside down behind the bar. I sat there thinking of what it used to be like when we stood on our heads years ago. All the blood rushed down to your head and you saw coloured spots inside your eyelids.

So I told the barman. "Those bottles probably hate it. All the whiskey is pressing down onto their little brains and God alone knows what they are seeing." From then on he spoke to me in the gentle measured tones you use to someone who has just appeared at your front door with manic eyes and a chainsaw.

It's not my fault. When I was going to shovel some more coal onto the fire, my brother used to go into hysterics. He told me I was breaking up happy little family groups of coal lumps. He called me a mass murderer. Then when I was about to dump a spoonful of sugar into my tea he spoke with deep feeling about all the tiny grains whimpering because they knew that this was the end.

I still apologise to envelopes before ripping them open. I try not to hear little Hermesetas going "Eeek!" before dropping them into scalding hot coffee. I hold a cigarette in my mouth for hours before I can bring myself to light it.

I kept getting the sack when I was working on the trawlers up in Scotland. When I thought that nobody was looking I used to throw crabs and prawns back into the sea as fast as we were catching them. I thought it was very important to throw them back quickly because otherwise they might never find their mothers and fathers again.

I was inspecting a carpet in Finglas market last Sunday morning. I asked the man if he thought that the fleas in my house would be happy living in it. He looked at me and didn't say a solitary word. You get that when you worry about binbags, whiskey bottles and fleas. You never really get used to it.

*

All Aboard The Beanbag

It was easy to keep myself warm when I lived in one-room flats and bedsits. I lit the Superser during the day and went to bed with my clothes on. Whenever I needed to go down the hall to the toilet I put on my hat and coat and scarf and gloves and I never stopped to talk to anyone.

I used to dream about living in a house of my own. The thought of taking off my clothes before I went to bed really did appeal to me. No more putting on extra pairs of socks or woolly hats or piling coats up on top of the bedding. No more phone chats in the hall with my breath coming out in frozen clouds. If I ever buy another house I will never make the reasonable assumption that the central heating works. Mine doesn't and I can't afford to get it fixed.

I've been living in this house for four years now and I'm still based in one room during the winter. Myself and my three cats eat and sleep and drink in the sitting room because that's where the fireplace is. There are no more fleas whizzing up into the air out of the carpet. It is too cold for them. They have either headed off to Africa for the winter or they've lit little fires of their own and they're not coming out again until the Spring.

Our sleeping arrangements are simple. I get onto the beanbag first and curl up in front of the fire. Then the cats snuggle up beside me in order of seniority. I cover the lot of us with a couple of duvets and say, "Good night and God bless everybody." Willow, Blackie and Hoot are much better than rubber hot water bottles because you don't have to fill them up with water and they never leak during the night.

Whenever I have visitors during the Winter they walk into my sitting room and bask in the heat. They say things like — "My goodness-what a lovely warm house." So I throw on another couple of logs as if to say — "To hell with the expense.' the Superser is going full blast and we're all sitting there with the sweat pouring off us. People are peeling off jumpers and shirts and gasping — "My word ...you can't beat a nice bit of heat."

If they leave the room for any reason the cold stops them dead in their tracks. The sweat freezes on their faces and when they come back in again the tips of their noses have changed colour. They usually crouch noiselessly in front of the fire and communicate non-verbally until their circulation starts up again.

I don't get many visitors between the months of October and April. I call it the lonely season.
*

A Monkey On My Drainpipe

11.00 a.m. I'm not the only person in Ireland who is lying in bed with the 'flu. I know that. But there is a monkey on the sill outside my bedroom window. It lives next-door and it has just shinned up my drainpipe. I need my rest, but I think that the monkey wants to come in. It is pounding on the glass with a little clenched fist and making chattering noises with its teeth. I don't think I'll ever get better.

11.15 a.m. Willow is fighting back on my behalf. He is sitting on the sill inside my window and spitting at the monkey. He is also whacking the glass with his paw. This is not helping my recovery. A loyal ginger cat and a Rhesus monkey insulting each other through my window. I think I'll take another disprin.

12.00 a.m. The monkey is now scampering around my roof and tugging an electric cable. I know this because the cable goes down past my window and it is writhing up and down. Willow is now spitting at the cable because he thinks that it's a long thin black snake or something. My temperature has just gone up by two points.

15.00 p.m. Things are getting steadily worse. I wandered down to my front door to get a breath of fresh air and couldn't help noticing a big stripy tiger outside my gate. I don't think it is going to shin up the drainpipe and bang on my window because three men have got it on the end of a rope. I think that they intend tying it to a tree. Now I've got a headache and my legs are all-shivery.

15.30 p.m. Fair play to the Gardai. They come around very quickly. Now there are three men, a big tiger and a group of Gardai outside my house. I'm not sure whether you can arrest a tiger or take it into protective custody or what. I don't know where the monkey has gone. If it has got any sense it's up on my roof hiding behind the chimney. If I had a good long ladder and somebody to hold the bottom of it for me I'd go up and join him.

15.40 p.m. It's a funny thing but you never really get used to jungle creatures outside your house when you live in Dublin 3. Last summer I was making a banana sandwich in my kitchen when I felt strangely uneasy. Then I turned around and noticed a baby lion outside my back door. It wasn't nearly as big as the tiger but I still didn't feel like going outside to pick a few flowers.

The snake in my coal bunker affected me in much the same way. I went upstairs, locked myself into the bathroom and had a good tremble.

16.00 p.m. The tiger is gone and so are the Gardai. If my temperature gets any higher I shall probably evaporate and flow down the walls. I think that I'll go back to bed for a while but I'm not going to look out through my window. A hippo or a rhino or something really huge like that would surely give me migraine and then where would I be?

*

Guard Dog Tingles

I was walking down to The Point Depot after dark. The Liffey was sullen and the silent docklands were eerie. So I started to hum 'Puff The Magic Dragon' softly to myself and pretended that my guardian angel was carrying a baseball bat.

A huge guard dog flung himself suddenly against a gate with a violent explosion of wild barks and snarls. I nearly jumped into the river with the fright. There was clearly no point in reasoning with him through the bars. His message to me was simple. ''If you come in here I will eat you.''

I wanted to say — ''Don't you snarl at me like that. I wasn't climbing up your gate or rattling a stick along your bars or anything.'' But I kept on walking. For all I knew he might be able to run up one side of the gate and down the other.

Whenever I get a fright like that I always feel electric tingles in the tops of my fingers and if I close my eyes I can see all sorts of bright coloured lights. I don't think it's very good for you. It wouldn't be very wise to drive a car or work machinery with tingles in your fingers and lights behind your eyes.

One hundred yards further on in the semidark and it happened again. Another manic guard dog hurled himself against another gate and this time my heart actually stopped beating for a couple of seconds. It didn't pound like they do in the novels. It just stopped completely and I thought to myself — "My God I am dead because my heart isn't working anymore."

The dog was barking savage insults and terrible threats and I said a silent prayer in my mind — "Please God, make my heart start beating again because if you don't I will be found here tomorrow morning still standing up even though I am officially dead."

I knew that I was alive again when I felt powerful currents of electrical power surging through my fingers. This time I ran.

I have no idea how many guard dogs and gateways are down there. I was running so fast that it was impossible to count them. But I do feel that there should be some sort of advance warning. A flashing light or a big luminous dog sign or something. A fright like that could kill you.

I know that guard rabbits wouldn't be much of a deterrent but I for one would honestly prefer them.

*

Press-ups For Pussy Cats

I didn't mean to upset the balance of nature. Nobody loves birds as much as I do. I even watch the US Open golf on television so that I can hear birds singing live from across the Atlantic. I sit there enthralled and think ... "ust imagine, all the blackbirds in Clontarf are sound asleep right now, yet there's one singing its heart out up a tree on a golf course in America." I even get very impatient when the commentators keep rambling on about golf and I can't hear the thrushes properly.

I never realised that the balance of nature is so delicate. I acted from the best possible motives when I cut back on my cats' rations. I even explained it to them. "Blackie, Willow and Hoot . . . just look at yourselves. The three of you are getting middle-aged spread and it's all my fault. Every time you even think about mewing I open another tin of food. From now on things are going to change around here, so tighten your little belts."

It was two days later that I started to find birds feathers scattered on my front door mat. I felt deeply upset. There are lots of trees near my house and the air is filled with twittering and chirping and the flutter of wings. I love it. And now thanks to me, three furry hunters have gone on the warpath and nothing with feathers is safe.

I put the three of them back onto full rations and decided to approach the problem from another direction. If it is possible to train circus fleas to pull tiny chariots and do backward flips, surely it is equally possible to persuade cats to do press-ups. I started with Hoot. He was sitting on the upstairs window sill which overlooks Vernon Avenue. That is where he likes to monitor the traffic flow. I climbed up onto my desk directly under the sill and lay down on my stomach. "OK Hoot. Now pay attention. I want you to rest your full weight on your front paws and rise up and down like this." I demonstrated a series of press-ups to him with a lovely regular rhythm. I didn't realise until I had finished that an excited group of people was pointing up and peering at the window. For the previous three minutes they had been witnessing my bottom rising and falling and God alone knows what they were thinking. I decided not to make matters worse by explaining that I was teaching Hoot to do press-ups. I think I'll just have to wait until they introduce 'Low Fat, Slim Line' cat food.

*

Close Encounter With A Caterpillar

I was happy he was wearing his winter coat. The little furry caterpillar was wriggling his way across the path on Vernon Avenue and the afternoon was bitterly cold. He was heading towards a garden wall.

"Hold on a second little fellow," I said. "Where do you think you're going? You'll never get over that without ropes and climbing boots. "

The little caterpillar didn't stop or answer me or anything. They don't speak our language and as far as I can be sure they don't have a working knowledge of it either. Caterpillars probably make their own little sounds and you'd need ultrasonic hearing to eavesdrop on their conversations.

I picked him up and he curled into a ball in the palm of my hand. "I'm doing this for your own good," I explained to him. "If I leave you on the path, somebody will come along with clumpy boots and squish you into the concrete and then where will you be.'"

It was a rhetorical question. They are the best kind of questions to ask caterpillars.

"Please don't be alarmed because in a couple of seconds you will feel yourself whizzing through the air. I am going to fire you in over that garden wall and because God is good you will most probably land in amongst some gorgeous heads of cabbage." His body gave a little twitch which I interpreted to mean — "Rock on Pat ... I'm gettin' to where I like it."

I did a countdown in a clear voice so that he would know when to brace himself. "5 ... 4 ...3 ...2 ... 1 ...go caterpillar go!" And off he went.

It was only when I was on the bus that I began to have second thoughts about his flight. Maybe that little guy was perfectly happy with where he was heading in the first place. Perhaps one of his pals had said to him — "I tell you what. Take a left at that high wall on Vernon Avenue and I'll meet you in underneath the first green gate."

Maybe he was setting off on his very first date with the caterpillar of his dreams. There he was, crossing Vernon Avenue humming a happy romantic tune to himself when some well-meaning human picked him up and fired him over a wall.

I feel fairly sure he didn't suffer concussion when he landed on the far side because his furry winter coat felt nice and bouncy. But I went into the garden and had a good look around on the

way home just to make sure. I honestly thought caterpillars went fast asleep or hitched off to Africa for the winter.
*

Highland Toffee

I never received a present like it before. A friend of mine came over from Scotland and she brought me a big box of Highland toffee. There was a little metal hammer in the box as well. It was the same sort of hammer with which you are exhorted to smash bus windows if you can't get out in a hurry any other way.

I removed the paper and whacked the toffee. I hit it a really good belt. There was a spectacular explosion and chunks of toffee whizzed around the room. Fragments shot into the fireplace and flew in under the table and one flat piece hit the ceiling and stayed there.

We ate all the bits that we could find. Then we unstuck bits from the bottoms of our shoes and we didn't eat them. The flat bit stayed on the ceiling for three days until the front door slammed in the wind. Then it fell down. My friend ate that bit.

Joan went back to Scotland two weeks ago. Her present lingers on. One big lump took up residence in Hoot's tail. He wasn't very happy about it. No self-respecting cat wants a huge piece of 'Mrs McTavish's Treacle' firmly attached to one of his waggy bits. One option was to fill a basin with warm soapy water and dangle his tail in it for a couple of hours. But I couldn't possibly answer the front door bell holding a soapy cat. "Eh, hello ...I'm just soaking Hoot's tail to get the toffee out." People have been reported for less.

Another option was to chew it out for him. "Hold still Hoot and don't be alarmed if you observe me chewing your tail ...believe me, it's for your
own good." But that would probably take a very long time so I would be obliged to change the out-going message on my answering machine. "Hello — I can't come to the phone right

now because I'm chewing Hoot's tail." People might never ring you again.

When I approached him with my scissors he fled upstairs and hid in the hotpress. I don't honestly blame him. "Hoot — I promise I'm not going to cut off your tail. You know me better than that. I just want to snip out Mrs. McTavish's stuff before you get stuck to a garden wall somewhere."

A very obliging friend held him and talked gently to him while I snipped away at his nether regions. "Don't worry Hoot — you could have much more drastic operations than this, believe me."

That kept him quiet for a while. There are far worse things for a tom cat than toffee in your tail.

*

Yappy Dogs, TDs And Vanishing Shop Assistants

10.00 a.m. It was time to take a stand. I've always been terrified of dogs. Big ones or small ones . . . it makes no difference. I'm convinced that they're going to bite me or eat me, or both. There's probably a scientific name for my condition like "Doggyfobis' or something. A little yappy dog raced out of a gateway in Vernon Avenue and insulted me with threats and menaces. Part of me was urging — "Run for your life." Another part was saying — "Stand your ground. You can't spend the rest of your life running like this." Very slowly I got down onto my hands and knees on the pavement. I rolled my eyes and followed up with a deep throated growl and three primitive snarls. The animal took to its heels and for all I know it is still running. It may even need the services of a dog psychiatrist but that is not my problem. He started it.

11.30 a.m. I came across an election leaflet while tidying my house. It's from a local politician and one sentence caught my eye because it is written in italics for emphasis. "Your problems are my problems." That is exactly what the man says. He has also very kindly given me his home address. Starting from next month I propose to forward all my telephone, ESB and mortgage demands to him. I fully intend to take him at his word. I've also got a problem about being fifty, but I don't think he can really help me with that.

12.30 a.m. I'm trying to find someone to help me in a modern Dublin department store. It's a lovely shop ...oodles of space and light and colourful displays but I can't see a shop assistant anywhere. Where do they all go? Every so often a girl in a blue overall appears for a split-second but before you can catch her eye she is gone again. Do they have official hiding places or trapdoors in the shop floor or what?

12.40 p.m. I'm looking at a girl in a blue overall who hasn't spotted me yet ... creeping past the jeans, in around the polonecks ...don't make any sudden moves. How did she do that? One second she was near the cash register as large as life and suddenly ...GONE! Perhaps the trainee manager beams them up through the ceiling.

12.50 p.m. At last. A smartly dressed young man in a dark suit is standing-beside the waistcoats. He is making no attempt to hide so I walked up and asked him — "Excuse me — do you have any bathing togs?" He said that he's got a lovely red pair at home buy why exactly do I want to know ... do I wish to borrow them or what? "I don't work here," he said with a hurt and offended voice. I think that everyone should be supplied with an 'I Don't Work Here' badge on entering a shop because you feel mortified whenever it happens. Scarlet isn't the word for it.
*

In Memory Of Demitrius

9am. Demitrius was lying on his back with his legs up in the air when I came into the kitchen. I hoped that he was only sleeping because I've never seen him like this before. I gave him a couple of gentle prods with a chop-stick but he still didn't move. I'm really going to miss him.

9.15am. I put some cotton wool into a matchbox and sadly placed Demitrius inside. I haven't got the faintest idea what sort of an insect he was. Kind of oval-shaped with two little peepy yokes at the front which he used for looking into rice crispy boxes. I think that he secretly wanted to be a free gift or something. He had six legs, all of which were bandy, so when he trundled across the kitchen table he looked like a central defender or a gunfighter.

9.20am. I said goodbye to Demitrius and closed the matchbox. I've only known him for about four days. He appeared in my kitchen out of nowhere and sort of hung around the rice crispy box. My three cats were very good about him. They never attacked him or ate him or anything like that. They just watched him walking around the place and let him get on with it. I don't think they knew what he was either. I suspect that he was a Black Oval-Shaped Bandy Legged Rice Crispy Peeper.

9.25am. I dug a big hole in the soil in front of my house because by this stage I had installed himself and his matchbox inside a large rice crispy box. Somehow it seemed right. I didn't even cut the Xtravision tokens off the side. Blackie, Willow and Hoot sat on the wall and watched me digging the hole. They have seen me doing some very strange things in my time but never before have I buried a rice crispy box.

9.40am. I felt that I should say something appropriate about the little insect because I really had come to love him wandering around my kitchen. John Wayne said some brilliant things over a grave in *The Cowboys* but he was burying some of his cowhands. This was different.

9.45am. I removed my hat, cleared my throat and spoke. "Demitrius, I have never met an insect like you before. I've had spiders and earwigs and beetles in my house but they never fitted in like you did. You never felt the need to show off by walking upside down across the ceiling or anything like that. I'm really going to miss you. I haven't got a clue where you're gone but if insects have got souls and I'm pretty certain that you have- I hope that you're surrounded by loads of rice crispy boxes. Goodbye and thanks for four great days. Then I shed a few tears and filled him in.

9.50am. I ate my breakfast but couldn't bring myself to have any rice crispies. Perhaps he has got a brother or a cousin somewhere. If they're ever looking for a kitchen, I hope they stumble into mine.

*

More Power To You Simon

I have never seen a cobweb like it. It seemed to drift between the branches of the hedge without actually moving. I stopped and looked at it for a long time perfect and fragile and silver because it was wet with the dew of the morning. I couldn't see the spider anywhere. I really did want to see him so that I could say, "Thank you for weaving such perfection outside my front door." But there was no sign of him. I couldn't believe that any spider would create such symmetry and then wander away before anybody could say congratulations to him. I think that it's a pity they don't sign their work when they are finished. All the great artists used to do that. All he has to do is spin his name at the bottom and put the date beside it. Something like — 'Simon spider the Third . . . August 25,1993.' Then we'd all know.

There was a little earwig hanging around the web. One of those guys with pincers at the back. I think this means that he has to go into reverse before he can nip anybody. He was loitering beside the web in much the same way that children sometimes sit down on the pavement beside a colourful chalk picture after the artist has gone. "Hey you," I said to him. "Come off it. You're not fooling me for one second. You don't spin webs like that. You just go around the place backwards nipping people with your pincers. Shame on you for trying to steal the credit for

Simon the Third's handiwork." The earwig knew that I was onto him. He scuttled in underneath a leaf and stayed there. Proper order. My taxi was due any minute so I scribbled a hasty note to Simon and left it beside his web. "Dear Simon, Thanks for giving me such a brilliant start to the day. I'm off to Galway to do a poetry reading and won't be back until the morning. Otherwise I'd leave my front door open and you'd be welcome to come in and spin some more of your groovy webs all over the house. Perhaps I'll see you tomorrow, Pat." Four hours later I couldn't believe my eyes. There in the branches of a tree outside Nun's Island Art Centre in Galway was another one of Simon the Third's webs. I recognised it. I'd know his style anywhere. I just know that it was his. I haven't got a clue how he got over to Galway so quickly. If I ever see him it's the first thing I'm going to ask him.

*

Dropping It On Daniel

I believe that trainee seagulls practise their bombing raids on Daniel O'Connell's head. Their squadron leader lines them up on a cliff-top out on Ireland's Eye. "Now listen to me. No tricky stuff at first. Forget all about moving targets for the time being. There's this brilliant statue just beside O'Connell Bridge. It doesn't move or anything, so off you go and may your God go with you."

I'm convinced that they are given exact map references because they never hit Jim Larkin or any of the other statues. Poor old Daniel O'Connell gets it every time. Perhaps the young gulls have never heard of Catholic Emancipation. Perhaps they don't care.

The crows who live up in the trees in the middle of O'Connell Street are much more civilised. I've watched them. They peep out over the side of their nests and collect bus numbers. Sometimes they fly down to the GPO and perch on the roof overlooking Henry Street. They like to check up on how many cigarette lighters are going for a pound down below.

They never drop anything on Daniel's head. They've got a sense of civic pride because they actually live in the street. They even hold their fire when they are directly over the Anna Livia fountain. They are an example to us all.

My heart goes out to our inner-city pigeons. Many of them are attending group therapy sessions on the open ground near Pearse Street Garda station. Their little nerves are shot to pieces. Through no fault of their own, they have been utterly unnerved by the new automatic road sweeping machines.

One North Earl Street pigeon was almost swept inside a lorry by the spinning brushes and suffered a complete nervous breakdown. He was the one who started the panic. He addressed an emergency meeting on Clery's roof and the damage was done.

"My dear pigeons, this is war. Those machines may look like road sweepers but that is exactly what Dublin Corporation wants us to think. Make one false move and those brushes will gobble you up ... one gulp and you are gone, man, gone."   An advanced seagull blitzed my bedroom window today. Because of the overhanging roof he had to make the same sort of approach run that The Dam Busters perfected. I am leaving it there as a tribute to his technique.

*

In Praise Of Cats

They won't chase after sticks and bring them back. You can throw sticks about and shout "Fetch" until you're blue in the face. The average cat will look at you with pity and amusement, yawn a couple of times and wander away in search of higher intelligence.

They won't sit or stay or do anything else that you tell them. They understand exactly what you wish them to do and pride themselves on always doing the direct opposite.

Cats can hear a fridge or cupboard door opening in the next parish. They don't believe in civilised arrangements like set mealtimes. Cats will effortlessly eat rings around themselves and then cheerfully steal your dinner.

Cats will sit on the edge of the table while you are eating a meal and completely ignore your plate. They will look the other way and convince you that nothing is further from their minds than the food which is in front of you.

Yet without appearing to move one inch they will be edging nearer and nearer to your plate. Turn your back for one second and your food is gone.

There is no such thing as a cat owner. It is not possible to own an animal which is doing you a major favour by living in your house.

Cats are the only creatures on four legs who have perfected the art of training human beings. They can get you to the stage where you leap out of a warm bed at 4.30am because you hear a meow outside the front door.

Cats are only ever interested in curling up and sleeping in the one place where you were intending to sit. You can move them if you like, but sooner or later the phone is going to ring and when you get up to answer it your place is gone again.

They know with absolute certainty which part of the newspaper you are trying to read. This is the only place in the whole house where they decide to sit. They also do this to letters you are writing, notes you are studying and pictures you are attempting to draw.

They will bring home presents to you of rats, mice, voles, shrews and assorted birds.   They are the most infuriating, independent, graceful, aristocratic beguiling creatures on four legs. From time to time they seem to think that we deserve them. You don't need a licence for a cat. Mankind wouldn't dare.

*

This Dog Could Change Your Life

I never rush into it with my few pence. I take my time and have a really good look at the greyhounds when they are led out onto the track. Firstly I cross off the ones who look worried about anything. If a greyhound has been dumped by her boyfriend she's certainly not getting my few pence. I try to select a dog who has got the whole thing sussed. You can very often tell this from its body language. Watch out for the kind of laid-back walk that says, "The sooner I get through this business of humouring the humans by chasing after a phoney hare, the sooner I'll get home to my bed." A clued-in dog like that can win you a fortune.

I've learned to disregard the people who walk up to you and speak out of the side of their mouth. The ones who go "Psssst" at you. There are always at least two or three "Psssst" people at the dog track. They begin by asking you which one you are backing. When you tell them, they roll their eyes backwards until their pupils disappear. Then they do a very loud hiss by breathing inwards in a huge hurry. They make you feel as if you have just said something terrible.

Don't listen to them, no matter how convincing they sound. Not only do these people know the owner, the trainer, the dog psychologist and the vet, but the greyhound itself regularly appears to them in private visions and confesses all its inner secrets. Tell them to go and take a running "Psssst" at themselves. Little children are much better. They know exactly what is really going on. They have heard Daddy talking to Mammy about their dog in the car on the way to the track. If the greyhound in question couldn't even win an argument, they have heard it straight from the owner's mouth.

I wish that it was possible to talk to the men and women who walk the dogs around the track before each race. I think that as soon as you hand over your few pence, you should be put in

radio contact with the one who is walking the dog. "Would you ever slow down a bit! You're wearing the poor thing out. Will you for God's sake let it sit down for a while and have a rest? Or better still, pick it up and carry it."
They don't have names like Rover and Spot. Greyhounds are called things like Garryhinch Whizzer or Parsimonious Pincher. They ignore people who yell "Sit" at them during a race. Proper order
*

Beware Of These Men

I was ambushed by a 'Health is Wealth' man this week. "Supposing that you win the Lotto and get promotion and marry the girl of your dreams all in the same week, but then you fall into a combine harvester ... it's no good to you. And do you know why?" I begged him to tell me. "Because you haven't got your health." Then he worked his way towards the pay-off by asking me the crucial question. "And what is health?" "Eh . . . banana?" I suggested. He shook his head vigorously. "No. . . No!" I tried another guess. "Eh . . . screw driver?" He was appalled by my total ignorance. "Your health is your wealth," he said. Then he wandered off to find another victim.
I met a 'Key In The Door' man on Butt Bridge. "It's not like in the old days," he said. "In the old days you could go away for the holidays and leave your wife's jewellery lying around the house and your life's savings hanging up in a sock over the mantelpiece and the key in the front door and there wouldn't be a bother on you." "But would you not be afraid of somebody getting into your house?" "Not at all," he said. "When you got back, the house was full of pots of home-made jam and freshly baked brown bread. The neighbours left them for you after they'd finished darning all your socks, sweeping your chimney and turning the collars on your shirts." "You had your health as well," I added. "And we all know what that is." The old man was delighted. Then I told him that you were even

richer if you had your mother's love because that is a blessing. He was overjoyed.

I met a 'Cold but Dry' man in Marlborough Street. They're the men who walk up to you and rub their hands vigorously together. "Cold!" Then another rub of the hands. A long pause. "But dry!" I told him that the cold kills all the germs which is just as well because if you win a fortune and catch pneumonia, the money is no good to you. "Now you have it," he said.

I met a 'Change from a Pound' man on the bus. "You could bring your wife out for a three course meal, go to the pictures, have a couple of pints, buy a box of chocolates, have ice cream in Cafollas, go home in a taxi and still have change from a pound," "And when you got home," I ventured. "The key was still in the door." I was just about to say — "But if you fell into a cement mixer ..." but I decided there is no sense in pushing it.

*

Stop The Lights!

I am learning lots of new and exciting things. If you buy a rubber bathing hat which is too tight for your head, you will see lovely coloured lights in front of your eyes. The new bathing hat locked onto my forehead like a vice. It was so tight I was afraid that my brain would pop out through my ears and upset the other people in the changing room. As I walked towards the pool I could hear strange music behind my forehead. It sounded like Johann Strauss being played much too fast on an electronic keyboard. I discovered that when I swam slowly the music synchronised itself to the rhythm of my strokes. It was just like enjoying all the benefits of a Walkman without actually wearing one. I told a man in the water beside me that my new bathing hat was creating music inside my head. He said that you don't get much of that nowadays. St. John of the Cross used to hear a choir of angels behind his forehead but he wasn't wearing a rubber bathing hat. I tried to loosen the rubber by stretching it away from my head. My wet hands were slippy and the hat whammed back against my forehead with a stinging smack which made my eyes go all funny.

I tried gently massaging the top of my head and the music dimmed as if somebody was just about to make an important announcement inside my head. I listened but nobody said, "And now we go over to the Met office." Nobody said anything. Then the coloured lights started. It was like the laser show that they had outside the Customs House. I could see spectacular bursts of green and red and orange. I'm quite certain that it can't be good for you. The flow of blood is probably being cut off from your brain and you could very easily develop a lisp or a strangulated hernia.

My father used to talk to me about priorities. I could almost hear him asking me: "Son, which is more important-keeping your hair dry or risking all your memory cells being wiped?"   I removed my bathing hat and a curious thing happened. It was just like when you switch off a vacuum cleaner and the motor goes right on whirring for a few more seconds. The music and the lights rocked on for a little while longer before fading to black. I miss them.   My new bathing hat is boring. No more high-speed Strauss. No more lovely lights. I've still got the other hat in the hot press. At any time I choose, I can treat myself to a psychedelic mixed-media show. It's great to know that.
*

A Cheap Miracle Cure With No Side Effects

It's very exciting when you discover something by accident. An apple falls on top of your head or you notice a spider getting something right at the seventh attempt. It's events like these that send people rushing down the road dripping with their own bathwater. They happen when you least expect them. I was finding it very hard to breathe last week. A combination of feathers in my bottom pillow, cats sleeping on my chest, and a sudden change in wind direction which blew all the pollen from

Mayo, Galway and Clare in through my kitchen window. I shook my inhaler and took in a deep draught of asthma medication. Suddenly I panicked, I could feel a foreign body entering my airways at high speed. "My God — I've sucked something solid in and it's heading straight for my lungs — I'm going to choke and die and I'll never know what it was."

I coughed and spluttered and fought for breath and something shot across the room. It pinged against the far wall and hit the ground. Suddenly my breathing was crystal clear again. I felt excitingly re-born. The little earwig on the floor probably felt the same way because it was still alive. It probably couldn't wait to get back to its pals and tell them where it had just been. "I have just gone where no earwig had ever ventured before so let's have a bit more respect around here."

I realise that the medical profession is very cautious. I have no problem understanding this. I do not expect them to rush headlong into print and advise pharmaceutical companies to include live earwigs in their inhalers. They like to check these things out first. Doctors would be understandably slow to write on their prescription pads - "Take two puffs four times daily and include an earwig in each one." Maybe it was a once off. A mere coincidence. But the facts are there nonetheless. An insect in the full of its health hurtles backwards into my bronchial tubes and before it even has the chance to look around it whizzes out again head first. Suddenly I'm breathing better than ever. Perhaps it comes under the broad heading of Alternative Medicine. Perhaps in years to come we'll all be inhaling them. So far I have not experienced any side effects. If I do you'll be the first to know.

*

Appendicitis Hardly Counts Any More

There was a time you got a bit of respect for it. Once upon a time your appendix really did count for something. I was visiting a friend in hospital last week. I was dying to know what everybody else was in for. "Ah, don't mind your man over there. He's only getting his appendix out." If you want to talk about your appendix or your tonsils now, it better be good. You need to be sailing single-handed around the world during a hurricane. The doctor is giving you step-by-step instructions by radio and you are using your cleanest galley knife. Doing it yourself still gets a bit of respect.

I've left it far too late. I should have had all my minor bits removed in the '50s. Triple-bypasses weren't even heard of then. If I was you, I'd get that one done as fast as you can. The glamour is wearing off. Old women at bus stops with their shopping trolleys had their triple-bypasses two or three years ago.

When my father had his appendix out, the whole house came to a standstill. He had the good sense to have the operation in 1956. We all sat around the kitchen table and shouted out things like, "A toothbrush ...two clean pairs of pyjamas ...a brush and comb!" My mother wrote everything down. Then we all co-operated on packing his bag. We even included my father's appendix in the family prayers. The entire household gathered at the front door to see him off. We held up the family pets so that they could see him off too. We made little impromptu speeches and hugged him and promised to be good. We even wrote the exact time of the operation on the calendar in the kitchen.

Hernias are ten-a-penny nowadays. Yet the man in the next bed to mine managed to get superstar status as recently as 1989. He had the wit to be drilling for oil in the desert when his hernia struck. He was bumped from oasis to oasis in the back of an emergency jeep. A friendly Bedouin mopped his brow with a Lawrence of Arabia T-shirt. This guy's hernia had definite style and the nurses loved it.

The basic problem with nervous breakdowns is that they are either major or minor. Even after six of them. I still couldn't break out of the minor league. I was saved by a Cork woman who had worked out her own brilliant rating system. "Listen boy-six good minors equals one spectacular major any day!" I embraced her. By that kind of reckoning six or seven thousand tonsils equals one triple-bypass. But where would you find that many tonsils?

*

Man Or A Mouse

The book told me to lie on in bed when I waken up. It told me to lie on for 20 minutes and repeat positive thoughts to myself. So I lay there chanting: "I am a good and worthwhile person." After about 10 minutes I had graduated to - "I can climb Mount Everest with a broken leg if I really put my mind to it." That was when Blackie, Willow and Hoot charged into the room. They surrounded the bed and mewed some hungry outraged thoughts of their own. "Come on Pat — shift yourself, our breakfast is 10 minutes late." I wandered downstairs and opened three tins of food, still chanting to myself: "I am a child of the universe, I have the right to be here." Then I went back upstairs and lay down again. I was still feeling a bit negative so I tried: "I am only a mouse when I think like one." My mouse feelings were just beginning to ebb away when the phone rang downstairs. " Hello Jack — did you get the lump hammer?" The voice at the other end didn't bother about checking the number or anything. It called me Jack and went straight into talking about lump hammers. " My name isn't Jack. You've got a wrong number." I was thrilled with the assertion in my voice. Not a trace of mouse. "Well, who's that then?" So I told him. "This is a child of the universe who is tapping into his power centre." The voice paused for a second, said "Rock on brother" and hung up. The book — now told me to throw open my bedroom window and fill up my spirit with the new day. I flung it open and very loud bells started to ring. A blue light began to flash on the wall outside. The book didn't say anything about switching off your alarm before you start. I raced downstairs and keyed in my number. Then I rang the central control to report a false alarm. If you don't do this immediately, your house will be surrounded by more flashing blue lights and Gardai with loudhailers. I wandered back up to the open window to fill myself with the new day. My first deep inhalation hit me with a sudden pain which almost doubled me up. I'm not really sure what happened but I think I may have cracked one of my ribs because something very definitely went click. I can't cough or sneeze or anything now because it hurts too much. In future, I think I'll just do the laying on in bed bit and let the new day fill somebody else up.

*

Season Of Prickly Heat, Winter Vests

We used to dread summer starting early. Our winter vests were rough and prickly. They buttoned right up to the neck so you had to keep your shirt closed as well. Otherwise your friends would know about the hickey old-fashioned yoke you were wearing underneath.

It was murder when May was flaming hot. The prickly bits seemed to come alive with the heat. "Ma — I'm roasting — can I get into my summer vest?" Left to her own devices your mother would have probably said yes. But your granny was sitting in the corner with all the weight of accumulated wisdom on her side. "One swallow doesn't make a summer." That was all she had to say. But she didn't just leave it at that. She always remembered some young lad from her part of the country who got into his summer vest with indecent haste. Two weeks later he was dead from an accumulation of pneumonia, bronchitis, glandular fever and rickets. His name was always Kevin.

"Ma — I'm dying with the heat. All the other lads have got their summer vests on." You could sense that she was wavering. Liberation from prickles was close at hand. But granny was still in her corner and she really knew how to shaft you. "Cast not a clout till May is out." That was the clincher.   Apparently granddad cast a clout or two while she was away in Dublin shopping for some more good prickly vests. She was only gone for a day but that was long enough for the poor man to plunge headlong into hot and cold flushes, dizziness, triple pneumonia and rickets. There was no point in saying "Ma — all the other lads have cast their clouts." Granny had spoken.

Going for a swim was worse. "You finished your dinner at exactly 23 minutes past one." She would say it to you with the sort of sepulchral voice you associated with bats, bubbling cauldrons and bodysnatchers. She remembered a healthy young slip of a lad who didn't wait for the full hour before getting into the water. Another thirty seconds and he would still be around. His name was Kevin too.

None of us had a watch so we used to sneak the alarm clock out of the house covered with a towel. We were afraid to even have a paddle until exactly twenty-three minutes past two. Then we'd all race down the beach, free from fears of cramps, jelly fish, tidal waves, killer whales and rickets.   The best thing about being grown up is that you can cast your clouts whenever you feel like it.

*

Go On Son, Get That Salt Into You...

Salt used to be something you dumped onto your fry until you could hardly see the food anymore. "Go on son -get that salt into you. You've just sweated tons of it out on the football pitch." So you bashed the bottom of the salt cellar against the table and shook showers of the stuff all over your food. Now you read the small print on the side of packets and do little sums.

I don't know where I am anymore. People gave us so much false information. "Would you ever stop moping around the house. Get out there and lie in the sun. Think of all that goodness you're storing up for the winter." Sometimes you'd

fall asleep on your towel. By the time you woke up again everybody had gone home ages ago and the tide was back out.

Frying pans were sizzling day and night. Eggs and rashers swimming in lovely grease. Thick wedges of white bread dripping with butter. Dessert spoons full of sugar dumped into gallons of tea. "That's right son — get it into you. Growing boys need their strength." The only things you were warned about were bad company and mixed marriages.

Now I worry about what they're going to tell us next. Every time I open the paper I see something new. I think that sleep is OK, but you can't be sure. Jogging used to be healthy but now it loosens your knee-caps. Nothing that they announce in future will surprise me.

"Warning ... speaking too much French can cause premature deafness and ringing noises the inner ear"... Caution ... holding hands in the pictures can lead to millions of microbes from the other person swarming up your arm and building tiny nests under your armpit."

There is no end to the scary stuff. Scientists are chuckling away to themselves in secret laboratories. "Why don't we scare the hell out of people who love a nice cup of tea? We'll tell them that tea makes your pancreas turn orange by interacting with your toothpaste ."

They love picking on all the little harmless things you enjoy doing. "You may believe that reading in bed leads to a relaxed night's sleep. We have just discovered that it sets up an energy field above your head which loosens the ceiling."

You probably thought that stamp collecting was an educational hobby. Under certain conditions it can cause severe moulting in racing pigeons and loss of form in champion greyhounds.

Dying is still OK. But they're working on it.
*

Don't Panic

I'm very lucky that I don't get major panic attacks any more. Those days are gone now and I don't have any problems about going out. Nowadays I only get ordinary little panics like, "My God, I think the driver has forgotten to tell me the stop I asked him for and now I don't know where I am and maybe I'll be lost forever and never find my way back to somewhere that I know." When the inspector gets on the bus and you can't find your ticket and your tummy gets a horrible sinking feeling, it is very important that you don't start turning out your pockets and tipping the contents of your handbag onto the seat beside you. It is far too easy to communicate your ordinary little panic to everybody else on the bus. Suddenly they're all hot-faced and flushed and frenziedly ripping things out of their pockets as well.

I hate the ordinary little panic I feel whenever I see a drunken man staggering towards me. They always grab a hold of my arm and ask me for money. When I tell them that I'm not giving them any, they start to shout and call me names and my legs go to jelly. On second thoughts that one is a big ordinary little panic. We all get the one like, "I think that I've been given the wrong change in this shop, but if I say something maybe it'll turn out to be the right money all the time and then where will I be?" I can just about handle that one.

I got a huge big ordinary little panic in Grafton Street during the summer. I was strolling along feeling the sort of safe secure glow that comes from believing that your asthma inhaler is in your pocket. A young busker rushed over to me and said "Thank God it's you — could I ever have a puff of your inhaler?" His face was tense and his breathing was troubled. "That is no problem. Just take it easy. There is nothing to worry about." Seconds later I was ripping my pockets inside out and searching the lining of my jacket and the pair of us were clinging to each

other and jumping up and down and shouting, "Don't panic, don't panic!"
I never ever go up off the ground in planes. That used to give me gigantic enormous huge big ordinary little panics. I hate them.
*

Setting My Bloodstream Free

The basic problem is my belt. It doesn't expand and contract with my stomach. After a good meal at home. I love to open it and unbutton the top of my jeans and ease the zip down a bit. I don't eat out much these days but when I did I felt a bit shy about opening up all of the hatches afterwards.

Granny was right. If she was still around I'd be the first to tell her. She said that belts were against nature. She said they held you like string around a sack of potatoes. Look at Granddad. His face is serene and relaxed. It is the face of a contented man who wears braces. The blood is able to flow up and down his body without having to squeeze past that bit in the middle.

That was part of the problem. We associated braces with granddad who wore collar studs and bicycle clips and gold *fáinnes.*

Elvis Presley didn't wear braces. He belted out Jailhouse Rock and held his jeans up with a leather belt. Even when he was wearing a jacket you just knew that there wasn't a twangy pair of braces hidden underneath. We were profoundly impressed but Granny wasn't.

"That man's blood still has to squeeze past the bit in the middle." she said. I pretended not to hear but her words ruined my enjoyment of all Elvis Presley's films. One part of me would be glorying in my hero rocking his way through King Creole. The other part would be thinking about his blood doing its best to squeeze past the middle bit.

I'm slowly coming round to the notion of braces again. Perhaps it's the ageing process. I don't really know. It has now become more important to feel comfortable than to look sharp and trendy. Now I can appreciate the wisdom of the old men we used to see on bikes. They didn't care who saw their braces. We were horrified. We were into rebellion. We couldn't relate to cycling around in public making a show of yourself like that.

Fair enough-some of us were still being forced to wear braces at the time but we had the decency to keep them hidden. Sometimes they were much too taut and hoisted your trousers ever upwards with a tension that made your eyes water. But we didn't show it. Sometimes your sister grabbed them and whammed the elastic back against your body. But we never flinched.

The wheel has just turned the full circle. I am ready for them once again. Rock on Granny — I am about to set my blood-stream free.

*

The Original Mister Cool

It's great. I have now got a valid reason to carry a sports bag with a towel sticking out of it. For years I've been watching these guys who come up the steps out of 'Keep Fit' basements. They always pause at the top and blind you with the glow that comes off them.

I'm still not nearly fit or anything like that but I'm swimming three times a week in an indoor heated pool. It's brilliant walking home afterwards with your bag and your towel and your hair greased back like a male model doing a deodorant ad in the jungle.

I'm only at it for a couple of months now and I still can't run for a bus without risking the paramedics. But it doesn't matter. All you have to do is walk on the balls of your feet and look as if you're holding back immense power. You groove along as if you are barely able to keep your latent explosive energy in check. I've worked on my walk in private. Anybody can do it.

Your whole demeanour says to the world "Stand well back because any second now I might decide to cut loose and this son of a gun doesn't take any prisoners". It honestly doesn't matter that you've got three different coloured inhalers in your pocket. It's all in the walk.

My body isn't all bronzed and tanned. Nothing like it. It's a lovely white colour which perfectly sets off my black bathing togs. I can only do the breast stroke but once again it's all in the way that you do it. Those guys who power up and down the pool are fair enough. I believe that the thinking woman prefers a man who looks like a coiled spring but chooses not to unleash his primitive majesty in public. I have worked in private on looking like a coiled spring.

I can't help noticing that nobody blesses themselves anymore before getting into the water. I think this has happened since the introduction of lifeguards.

When we were kids on the beach there was no such thing. So you blessed yourself to make sure of going straight to Heaven.

Nobody calls them swimming togs anymore either. That went out with lumber jackets, fully fashioned nylons, school caps and shell cocoa.

One of these days I'm going to go down to the deep end. But I need to work in private on looking unworried first. I know the way my mind works. It will only start telling me: "Try not to panic but you are out of your depth ...My God ...put your foot down now and you are gone."

You have to wear a bathing hat in the pool which is great because nobody gets to see your bald spot. I think we should wear them all the time.

*

Without My Glasses

I saw a sign in a restaurant recently. I thought it said 'Hairy Pigs'. Common sense told me no restaurant in its right mind would put up a sign like that. So I put on my reading glasses and looked at it again. Now it read 'Buggy Bay'. I preferred it the first time. My eyes have gone to hell on me. When I look at words without my reading glasses I see the most amazing things. Last week I was trying with great difficulty to read a menu without them. "My goodness" I thought. "I've never heard of deaf coffee before". So I asked the waitress. "Excuse me," I said. "I'm quite certain you aren't serving coffee which is hard of hearing. Will you kindly tell me what those words really say?" The answer was as simple as 'decaff coffee'. "Sorry to bother you again but I feel equally sure you aren't dealing in bearded chickens." "You can bet your life on it," she replied. The chickens were in fact 'breaded'.

There is a metal bridge over the Liffey on the way down to Heuston Station. Whenever I pass it on the bus I seem to see the word 'Rimpindumble' and a date printed on the girders. I plan to walk down there later this week with my reading glasses on and check it out. Once again, I shall probably prefer it the first time.

My right arm is not long enough. Sometimes when I can't find my glasses and I need to read a telephone number in the directory, I hold the book out as far away from my eyes as I can manage. But it's still not far enough. Another 1' 3" and the letters would be crystal clear. I would like some enterprising manufacturer to come up with an extension which I can attach to my arm. Ideally it should be adjustable and telescopic because I estimate that my eyesight is failing at the uniform rate of one inch every year. By the end of this decade, if I am spared, I shall be holding the phone book clamped on the end of a vaulting pole.

All my bits are wearing out. I hear funny little clicking sounds in my knees when I walk. My left arm has almost given up the ghost. The only place on my entire body where I still have black hair is inside my nostrils. I have spoken to it. I've said — "You're not much use to me in there. Kindly get on top of my head where I really need you." But it ignores me. I suppose that given time, hairy pigs, deaf coffee and bearded chickens come to us all.

*

I'm Sure That Stomach Wasn't There Yesterday

When we were kids we took our flat tummies for granted. Our stomachs never cost us a thought because we had nothing to hold in. We talked to girls without the slightest bit of muscle strain. We didn't have to wear baggy shirts or anything. You could concentrate all your energies on making an impression. We oozed confidence because there were no bulging bits in the front. Our quiffs dripped with oily Brylcreem and we drawled cryptic phrases which we learned from Rowdy Yeats in Rawhide. His stomach was flat too.

I think I first started to hold mine in around about the time of The Beatles. The denial came first. "That extra bit has got nothing to do with me. I've never seen it before in my life. It must belong to somebody else." Then I stood in front of a mirror and thought — "My God — there must be some mistake. That mirror is going straight back to the shop. It clearly doesn't know the first thing about the male body."

John Lennon was my favourite Beatle. When he entered his roly poly tummy stage I really did believe he was doing it specially for me. I could almost hear him saying to Brian Epstein — "That guy Pat is going through a bad time with his extra inches so I'd better lash on a bit extra around the middle to make him feel better." My mind began to feed me all sorts of false information. "Ah sure you're grand. What's an inch or two between friends? I mean — just look at the state of that guy over there ... how could anybody let themselves go like that?" Then I looked in the mirror again. AAAAAAAHHHHH!!!

I used to feel like I was getting off with girls under false pretences. All the time my stomach muscles were working overtime. "I wonder would she still hunger after me if I left the brakes off. Maybe I'll do it a millimetre at a time over the next month. That way she'll never notice."

Past pupil reunions are brilliant. Twenty or thirty guys all concentrating like mad on their stomach muscles. A room full of acute waistcoat button tension. You long for a sign on the wall which reads — "This room is a specially designated stomach sanctuary. Feel free to let the brakes off lads as soon as you hear the beep." Then at a given signal, there is a lovely simultaneous flop. Oh, the relief of it. Bald spots are a million times better. They're the back where you can't see them.

*

People Who Look Their Age Are Less Confusing

So what is wrong with looking your age? Where is the crime in being sixty-something and looking it? I've never yet met an old person who said — "Isn't it great — I'm perfectly in tune with nature ... seventy two today and that's exactly how I look." I met an American woman last summer and the real her was in there somewhere trying to find its way out. She put me in mind of the GPO after they had sandblasted it and renovated the statues on the top. You know that the building is ancient but you can't quite put your finger on any of the old bits. Her voice sounded like my granny's but her hair looked like a stick of re-conditioned candy floss. She could almost have been Cher who had just boogied out through the wrong end of a time tunnel. It was very confusing. I didn't know whether to give her my seat on the bus or say, "Yo — the time is right for dancing in the street." I would like to have a quiet word with Cliff Richard. Let it go Cliff and give us all a break. As long as you insist on prancing around inside that golden aura of yours, we've got no chance of coming to terms with all our wrinkly bits. Every time I set my eyes on you I spend the next hour in front of the mirror massaging my forehead.

We've been led to believe that old is to be avoided at all costs. Disc jockeys dedicate records to venerable senior citizens and tell them that they are "one hundred years young". I very much doubt whether I'll believe that when my teeth are long gone, my grandchildren are semi-retired and I can only see my dinner with the aid of a magnifying glass.

I told a man yesterday that I'm forty nine. He said would you ever go way outta that — you don't look a day over thirty. There and then I would have happily changed my will in his favour. There's no better way of getting a total stranger to really like you. Simply ask them their age. Don't believe a word of it when they tell you. Express utter astonishment. "My God — you couldn't possibly mean it — sure you're only a teenager." They will die for you.

Old age pensioners are now called senior citizens. We've still got people who are called granny and granddad. I hope we always will.

*

Why Do They Do This To Me?

I wish that elderly people wouldn't keep doing it to me. We've just met and we're having a lovely chat. They're telling me lots of fascinating things about horse drawn traffic and Sackville Street and ten pints of Guinness for a penny. We're getting on like a house on fire and if we parted company right now they'd go straight home and say, 'I met this lovely man on the bus.' The question comes when you least expect it. "What age would you say I am?" You feel like a stick of dynamite with a slow burning fuse has just been inserted under your seat. One guess is all you're going to get and you better land at least five years under the right answer. "Well, I tell you this much for starters. You've got the crystal clear memory of somebody half your age. In fact, when my grandmother was twenty years younger than you she had the hazy recollection of someone thirty years older although you look about fifteen years younger right now than she did back then and she had a walking stick." You can feel the fuse getting shorter by the second.

"Ah no. Come on. you can tell me. What's a little guess between friends? I mean — its not as if you're going to hurt my feelings or anything. What age would you put me at?"

You're working things out in our head like this lady has the free travel but eh granny had that for twenty years or so ... eh, think of a number between sixty-five and eighty, take away ten and eh ...

"Do you know what I'm going to tell you? A very wise man once said, I think he was a Greek philosopher or something, he once said, you're as young you feel and if you feel ten years older than you really are right now I'd still knock about fifteen off it which actually puts you at five years younger, give or take a couple of months." And that is about as much kicking to touch as you are going to get.

"OK OK I'd say eh ... I'd say you're over the sixty-five mark anyway."

"Oh, you would. Over sixty five. How far over then?" The subtle change in the voice says you're on your last chance brother. Your only hope now is to pin it as close to sixty-five as makes no difference. "Eh sixty-five and one month and not a second older."

"Not at all. Would you go way outta that. I'm seventy-two." Thanks be to God. Saved. You live to stall another day.

Children wear little badges which boast 'I am 6'. We should all be obliged to wear badges like that by law.

*

Betrayed By My Innards

My insides are trying to get out again. The doctor in the hospital told me. I coughed every time he asked me to and he crouched down to keep a close eye on what was happening.

After a little while we got a sort of a rhythm going. Every time I coughed he said "Hmmmm."

"Cough … hmmm … cough …hmmmm…" If we'd started to click our fingers as well, we'd have got the whole outpatients' section on their feet dancing.

It wasn't as serious as the last time. My insides made an escape attempt six years ago but the surgeon put a stop to their gallop. Not only did he stitch up the escape route, but he put in a bit of plastic as well.

The County Council used to use concrete in Malahide when the sea was coming in too far. The doctor in The Mater preferred plastic, thanks be to God. He didn't tell me what colour the plastic was and I completely forgot to ask him. I hope that it's blue because it will match my veins.

I was mildly disappointed when the doctor in Beaumont told me that I don't need an operation this time. I was going to ask them to take a colour picture of my plastic bit with a Polaroid and then I'd know.

It is reasonably OK to admit to having a hernia nowadays because soccer stars over in England sometimes get them. Strikers and sweepers … guys who score with diving headers at Wembley. They are now coming out of the hernia closet. so I don't feel too bad about it.

What really does upset me is the thought that my insides aren't happy with where they are. I mean, what the hell is wrong with them? It's lovely and warm in there and I regularly send down good nourishing food and hot drinks.

I tried a holistic sort of approach by actually confronting my stomach and lower regions and giving it to them straight. I didn't use emotional music in the background because I wasn't aiming for overkill. I just wanted to tell my inside bits exactly how I felt about them.

"I feel very hurt and, yes, betrayed by the way that you're all carrying on in there. You don't see me trying to get away from you. I bring you to soccer matches with me. I take you on the

bus and everywhere. My God, you don't know when you're well off. I'll have a little less of the rebellious stuff from now on or I might just be tempted to take the concrete to you."
My insides haven't even rumbled since. That's the way to have them.

*

When You Mind My House For The Weekend

HELLO and welcome. We'll be back late on Sunday night. Here are a few things you need to know. Always open the fridge door nice and slowly, otherwise the carton of milk will shoot out and flood the kitchen floor. If this does happen, the cats will do most of the mopping up for you. Don't worry if the bathroom light suddenly goes off by itself. It does this. It will turn itself on again in its own good time.

The burglar alarm will probably ring while you are in the bath. I'm not sure why it does this. Possibly because the bath is loose and keeps whacking against the wall while you're washing your back. Try sitting still and don't make any sudden moves. If a girl called Jenny rings tell her the kittens are all gone.

The cats will mew to come into the house as soon as you have gone to bed. You can outwit them by simply going through the motions. Don't get undressed. Just turn off the bedroom light and stand in the darkness for about three minutes. Don't worry if you hear funny little beeping noises from my desk during the night. This is my stopwatch. I've only just bought it and don't know why it does this. I think it is timing laps or something. The back left plate on the cooker works on the same principle as the bathroom light. Hoot the kitten only eats Pilchard Whiskas. Willow the ginger cat will only eat his food on top of the fridge. Blackie will eat anything including everybody else's dinner. If Hoot climbs up to the top of the curtains and mews to get down, don't be fooled. He is perfectly able to do this himself. Don't assist him or you will spend the rest of the weekend doing it. If

the front door won't open for you give the bottom of it a good sharp kick.
Sorry all the food in the house is low fat, slim-line. sugar free. That's the way things are here at the moment. It's murder. I hid a couple of chocolate bars for myself but I can't remember where. If you can track them down they're yours. Try not to worry if you hear mini-stampedes during the night. Burglars do not chase one another up and down the stairs. The cats do.
If anybody calls looking for votes send them next door.
*

Do You Know Where Your Stopcock Is?

It's two years now since I moved into the house. I still don't know where my stopcock is. If a plumber asked me I wouldn't have a clue. It honestly never cost me a thought until I read the following authoritative statement in a women's magazine. "Everybody should know where their stopcock is." I think it's high time that I found out.
I was thinking about holding a "Find The Stopcock" party. Invite lots of friends around. After they have eaten all the crisps out of my cornflake dish they can have the time of their lives hunting it down. It could catch on in a big way. We could take it in turns to go to one another's houses and eat crisps out of dishes. Then we could track down each other's stopcocks.
It's funny the way you always think that you are the only one. When I was all shy and unsure of myself I used to believe that. It's probably exactly the same with stopcocks. I was sitting on the bus giving everybody else credit for being cool and calm and utterly in control.
Suddenly I had a deep and wondrous insight. Supposing I unexpectedly   shouted   —
"Hands up everybody on this bus who doesn't know where their stopcock is!" Mind you, they probably wouldn't admit it but you might just get one or two.

My father knew. So did my mother. The very moment that water began to cascade through the ceiling he used to shout — "Eileen ... turn off the stopcock!" My mother would immediately disappear in under the sink. Simultaneously my father would race around the house turning on all the taps and wildly flushing the toilet. They were a great team. They were brilliant. But I've looked in under my sink. There's nothing in there except a white plastic U-bend and six tins of catfood. God alone knows where the builders put it. If I ever get involved in house purchase again, I don't want to know about solicitors, surveyors and all that other stuff. I just want a map of the house with a huge big "X" on it. That's basically all I want to know.

Once upon a time I used to look at photographs of famous people and wonder what they looked like as a baby. I now find myself gazing at pictures of Bono and Tom Cruise and the Queen of England and thinking to myself — "I wonder if they know where their stopcock is." You can turn on as many taps as you like. Outside of this knowledge there is no salvation.

*

Don't Anyone Go Near That Switch!

I always expect to die when I'm changing a light bulb. I can never remember whether the light is switched on or off. Over the years I have tried to memorise little chants which will save my life. "Landing light, down is on, up is off." But there are two switches for that one, the ups and downs get all mixed-up and I don't know where I am.

We were given lots of dire warnings about electricity when we were little. We were told about children with metal knitting needles who were vaporised. We were told about disobedient kids who disappeared in a bright blue flash before they even had the chance to say goodbye to their mammies. The warnings were so graphic that for a long time I was afraid to even walk past a socket in the wall. I confidently expected a bolt of white light to whiz out and reduce me to a little mound of white powder.

The whole family used to stand around and watch when my father climbed up onto a chair. He never knew whether the light was on or off either. The tension was white hot because he approached the bulb like an army bomb-disposal expert who has just noticed a live mine floating in his bath. We were afraid to even breathe. My mother held the new bulb and we held our breath and as my father eased his hand around the old bulb. I used to say silent prayers. "Please God my father has promised to bring us all to the zoo tomorrow so don't let there be a bright flash because he might change his mind." He used to clench his teeth while he was easing the old bulb out. Sometimes the light shade would come away as well and slide halfway up his arm. I could never figure out how this was always my mother's fault because she was standing on the ground and hadn't touched anything. But somehow it was. She would say things like "Careful!" and he would say "I am being careful" and none of us laughed no matter what happened because we all wanted to go to the zoo.

It's much harder when you live on your own because there is nobody to blame when little bits of plastic come away in your hand. I still believe that certain parts of the light fixture are capable of blowing me and the chair into kingdom come but I don't know which bits they are. So I always wear rubber gloves and take my rings off just in case. My granny told me that a candle started the Great Fire of London. Do you ever know?

*

Cut Off In My Prime

EVERYBODY assumes that you've got one. The man who came to cut off my cable assumed it too. There he was standing at my front door with his little clippers at the ready. I told him that I didn't own a television. He said that's as maybe but look up there, that's our cable and if you don't pay your arrears you'll be getting the grand order of the snip to go with it. It's a great exercise in humility to close your eyes, surrender to your fate and gently murmur the words — "Snip me." You feel so much better after it. I asked him would he ever throw down the tennis balls from the gutter while he was up there and have a peep in under the eaves to see if the swallows have hatched out their eggs yet. I never knew that the people who lived here before me had the cable. The man said that was neither here nor there. He had a job to do. I could see from his face that he was really a compassionate snipper at heart. If you got him on a good day he'd go up his ladder with the clippers in one hand and a bucket of water in the other so that the neighbours would think you were only getting your windows cleaned.

I have never liked the idea of total strangers looking into my bedroom through the upstairs window. There are some things you like to keep to yourself and the colour of my pillowcases is one of them. To make matters worse Blackie is in the wardrobe right now with her newly born kittens. The last thing I wanted her to see was a strange man gawking in through the window with a pair of clippers in his hand. Cats have moulted out of season for less.

The man was up his ladder but there was nobody holding the bottom. I rested my foot against it to show there were no hard feelings and he said he'd do his best not to look in at my pillowcases and we were getting on like a house on fire.

I've got a wire brush and a bad head for heights so I asked him "If I pass out the brush would you ever mind scraping the rust off the gutters. I can give you a smog mask for your face because the bathroom is full of them and I've loads to spare."

He said it had been a pleasure to cut me off even though I don't have a television. I thanked him for the six tennis balls and the wire brushing. There are three baby birds in the nest. Isn't life great?
*

Doubt And Trembling

The light outside my front door blows up every time it rains. I've got quite used to it now. The light on the landing explodes in a different way. It blows up every time I put a bulb into it. The first time it happened I almost went into bronchospasm with the fright. I've now left a box of matches and some candles at the top and the bottom of the stairs. Exploding bulbs can trigger off self-doubt, trembling and all sorts of other psychiatric disorders. Candles are much easier on your nerves and they throw lovely shadows on the walls.

The light over my washhand basin in the bathroom used to go on when you pulled a little string. Then one day two plastic bits fell into my shaving water and the light went out. I dried my hands and fitted the bits back on again. The light then only worked if you pulled the string and hit it a sudden belt with your fist.

One day I hit it too hard and lots more plastic bits fell into my shaving water. Now it doesn't work at all but makes funny little spluttering noises when you pull the string. You get used to that. My sister has got a washing machine which says "Heinrich" over and over again. I prefer the splutters.

I thought it would be great to live in a house. No more bedsit horrors where the shower sometimes switched unexpectedly to icy cold and stifled your sex-drive for a month. No more queuing up with fivepenny pieces to use the phone in the hall. At least the lights worked. They may have been on a time-switch but they did work. The light in my toilet goes on and off all by itself whenever it feels like it. I've never had an electrical system like that before. I think it's because the bulb is hanging down from the ceiling on a piece of wire. I didn't swing from it or anything like that. I just woke up one morning and there it was dangling down. I warn my visitors when they go in to the toilet after dark. "Please don't be alarmed if you are suddenly plunged into darkness. It's not me outside at the switch.

Honestly. It just does that. Sit tight, be patient and it will come on again when it is good and ready." I bought a torch for £1.99. I tell my visitors that when they reach the top of the stairs by candlelight they will find it on top of the cistern in the toilet. I've left spare batteries beside it. You can't be too careful.

*

Little Frozen Slivers Could Blind Somebody

I honestly never knew that ice is so hard. I have bent knives while hacking away at the glacier inside my fridge. There is so much ice in there at the moment that I can't even close the little plastic door on the top compartment. It has been forced outwards by a creeping mass of expanding ice.

I usually make a start with my hairdryer. It's great for softening up the main glacier but it sometimes takes days. Long days of sitting on the kitchen floor directing a flow of warm air into the frozen waste. Long days of sitting and wondering, "Where in the name of God did that polar ice-cap come from?" Then I switch over to my hammer and screwdriver. I feel like an Alpine mountaineer who is chipping out little footholds for himself. It is very important not to allow anybody else into the kitchen while all this icehacking is going on. Little frozen slivers are whizzing around all over the place and they could easily blind somebody.

At the moment I am steadily working my way in towards a plate with a lump of steak on it. The ice at the top and bottom of my little freezer compartment has welded itself together and entombed the plate. The whole mass is trapped and frozen solid. I shall probably have to chip away for a couple of days before I even reach it. One ill-timed whack with the hammer and bang goes my good plate.

I have no idea where so much ice comes from. It starts gradually like a lovely sparkling frost. I keep saying to myself, " I Really must defrost that fridge soon." And then I go and do something else. The frost turns into ice and the available space inside my freezer section gets smaller and smaller. I know why I keep putting it off. All that ice is actually frozen water in disguise. It's not the sort of water that you can aim at anything. It doesn't flow obediently into saucepans or buckets. It prefers to drip and slop and overflow from plastic trays. It makes you wash your kitchen floor. Not because you want to, but because there's frozen water and lumps of ice everywhere you look.

Whoever designed the plastic tray for my fridge knew exactly what they were at. They worked out in advance precisely how much water any given fridge can produce. Then they designed a tray which is only capable of holding one-hundredth of it. The final flourish was to build in an aerodynamic wobble which spills the lot while you're walking to the sink.

When we were little, my mother used to bury the bottles of milk in a saucepan in the back garden. That woman knew exactly what she was at.

*

If people start to move the chairs in my house they will find all the cheaty bits. I couldn't be bothered painting behind things, so I go right up to the edges with the brush and then I stop. That is why one of my skirtingboards is now purple over as far as the wicker chair, and then cream-coloured in behind it. In future I shall ask my visitors to refrain from either moving their chairs or looking down behind things.

I don't know whether orange and purple go together but they do now. The door in my sitting room is bright orange and perfectly sets off the table, which is the same shade of purple that bishops wear. I don't for one moment expect to open my front door and find a bishop asking me if I'm coming out to play; but if this does happen I can bring him in and stand him beside my table and we'll have a perfect match. If the bishop is being chased by infidels with pointy spears he can also stand beside my front door and merge into it because that is now purple as well.

Some people buy little rubber footprints and coloured fishes which they stick to the bottom of the bath. I don't need to do this because Hoot walked along my window-sill while the paint was still wet. Then he rambled up and down the bath and left gorgeous pink paw-marks behind him. They're lovely. My brother gave me a present of a cream-coloured portable television. It has now got perfectly matching sets of lime-green paw marks on the top. That was Blackie. She sprang up on the window-sill and landed on fresh green paint. Then she obviously   thought   —
"I won't do the bath because Hoot has already done that in pink." So she wandered downstairs and little bits of carpet fluff stuck to her paws. This is why the footprints on top of my television are fluffier than the ones in the bath.

I painted some of the saddle-boards in my house sky-blue. At this stage, Willow was wandering around the place feeling very left out because he was the only cat without coloured paws. So I built little bridges over the saddle-boards with books and sheets of cardboard to keep him off the paint. He registered his protest by sitting on the bishop's table. I don't know whether ginger hair and purple go together. They do now.

*

Cracks, Creaks And Bleeps

I wish that my house wouldn't make sudden cracking noises in the middle of the night. One minute all is quiet. I'm Lying in bed feeling reasonably safe because I've said my prayers and the light is on. Without any warning a ceiling or a floor releases an unmerciful **crack** and I'm sitting bolt upright thinking — "My God ... what was that?" Sometimes my stairs creaks at two or three in the morning. All by itself. That scares me even more. I have no problem whatsoever with staircases which make noises when somebody is going up or down. You more or less expect that. But creaks when nobody is there can only mean Bogey Men with glowing coals where their eyes should be, or anaemic women in wispy veils who bite your neck if you're not wearing a scapular.

A sudden "bleep" from the bathroom nearly frightened me to death last night. I haven't got a clue where the water came from because the tap was turned off. It was an echoing kind of a bleep that you hear in dungeons where Sir Jasper's skeleton is chained to the wall but he still goes for rambles when nobody is looking.

When I was buying this house it never occurred to me to ask the auctioneer "And tell me does this property suffer from creepy cracks, eerie creaks or delayed bleeps in the middle of the night?" He probably wouldn't have known anyway. I believe that any prospective house-buyer who wants one should be supplied with a cassette recording of the building. The tape can be titled "What This House Sounds Like On The Inside Between The Hours of Midnight And Nine In The Morning." I was lying awake last week and I'd swear that the staircase and the ceiling were talking to each other. The stairs started it with a scary creak. "How's it going there ceiling? What sort of a day did you have?" The ceiling responded with an expanding crack. I was just about to sit up in bed and yell "Would the pair of you ever keep it down out there-I'm trying to get some sleep!" But once you start intimidating ceilings and stairs it's only a matter of time before you're racing into the bathroom to threaten the tap.

I know one woman who truly believes that the radiator in her bedroom is trying to seduce her with throaty gurgles. "It only talks to me when my husband has gone to the toilet," she said. You sometimes get that.

*

Nephews Should Let Their Uncles Win Games

I love to see young children doing it. I love to see them throwing sticks up into chestnut trees. As yet there is no video game called 'Hunt the Conker'. They've still got to get out into the fields and the parks and lash the sticks up as hard as they can.

My nephew always asks me as soon as I get to his house. "Would you like to play a video game Uncle Pat?" If I say no I'm a coward and if I say yes I'm on for another hiding. He is able to talk on the phone with one hand and gobble up electronic aliens with the other.

I can't even beat him at Video Snooker. On a real full-sized table I can swerve the cue ball and slam the black into the far corner pocket. Sitting on the floor beside my nephew I keep saying "Good shot David" through clenched teeth and secretly thinking — "That's your next year's Christmas present gone, pal".

It's no bother to them. They can change the time on your digital watch with a pin before you can say — "When I was your age we had a bit of respect." They express surprise that you are still using a portable typewriter and ask you awkward questions like do you prefer the Commodore or the Apple?

Nephews have never heard of Curly Wee and Gussie Goose, Stanley Matthews, The Kennedys of Castleross or Ruby Murray. They go through your entire record collection in thirty seconds and offer to loan you their CDs as soon as you invest in a decent sound system.

One of my uncles was a chain smoker. If I had said to him — "I would appreciate you not smoking in the same room as me because I have no wish to be a passive smoker in my own home," I'd have been sent up to bed without any tea. If I had asked my uncle for his thoughts on the condom debate my pocket money would have been frozen for the rest of the year.

In my day, cocaine was something which was administered to you by the dentist. Big clumsy boots were only ever worn by County Council workmen and you wouldn't have been seen dead in a pair of raggy jeans. Ozone was something that old ladies inhaled on the seafront in Bray and outer space belonged exclusively to Flash Gordon and Dan Dare. In my day your uncle gave you sixpence and told you to finish your dinner
*

You Have To Be Shouting At Something

Summer is a desperate time for these men. I saw two of them in a pub this week. The same men who yell expert advice all winter long. They were just sitting there, listlessly watching a soccer match on the television. A Brazilian player missed an open goal. He should have buried the ball but he booted it miles wide. If this had happened up in Dalymount Park during the winter, they would have earnestly advised him to sell his boots and donate his body to medical science. They would have passionately urged him to go home and get his granny. The two men just sat there and didn't react. The soccer season has only just ended and already their confidence is gone. I felt like talking very gently to them. "Come on lads. let's have a bit of the old fire. I still believe in you. It won't always be like this, honestly. You have to keep in practice." They just stared at the screen: two passionately articulate experts with nobody to shout at. It was a deeply moving moment.
I have heard these self-same men at the height of their considerable powers. I have heard them ardently suggesting to a referee that he place his whistle between two slices of brown bread and eat it. When feelings were running dangerously high, I have heard them begging an innocent linesman to attempt the physically impossible with his luminous flag. These men are simply surviving the summer with a melancholy resignation. They know that cricket matches are out of the question. If they

were living in Trinidad, they could dress up in colourful shirts and play 'You'll Never Walk Alone' on steel drums.
But cricket isn't like that in Ireland. No matter how much you may feel like it. you don't exhort the batsman to get the lead out. Soccer referees half-expect you to offer them the address of a good and understanding optician, but cricket umpires wouldn't stand for that kind of well-meaning feedback. Some wives are already deeply disturbed by the change in their menfolk. "Darling, please go downtown and shout at somebody. Find a good roadworks hole or something and shout advice at the men with the shovels. Stand at the bottom of a painter's ladder and offer him creative advice as only you can." But the men just shake their heads. It has to be a soccer stadium or nothing. Perhaps we could open up Dalymount or Tolka Park one night a week during the summer. The men could go along and roar things like '"Mind your house" at the seagulls. You have to be shouting at something.
*

Heading Up To *Dalier*

14hrs. I don't know what made me say it. We were getting on so well. Me and the two men waiting for a bus up to Dalymount Park to watch Bohemians. Talking about football. Discussing the exploits of the Republic of Ireland. Suddenly I heard a voice which I recognised as my own saying "Give a lot of that squad a blank map of Ireland and ask them to mark in Athlone, Sligo or Cork and they'd have to ask their grannies.
14.02. The two men were making strangling noises but they weren't saying any actual words. My voice kept right on going: "Put some of the Republic squad down in Dorset Street on the day of a big match and tell them to find their own way to Lansdowne Road and half of them would finish up in Kimmage." Now the two men were saying words none of which I can write down here.

14.10. This is much more like it. Heading up the North Circular Road by bus on a Sunday afternoon just like I used to do with my father. Back in the fifties when O'Connell Street was jammed with buses marked 'Football' and corporate tents hadn't been invented yet.

14.25. I love standing outside the stadium before it is open. Watching the players arriving with their club blazers and their kitbags. An old man is giving out to me for abandoning children's television. I'm explaining to him that what I really wanted to do was play for Bohs. I should have been a goalkeeper dressed in black who dived around the place and organised defensive walls and swapped shirts with Pele.

14.45. I never take it for granted that I'm sitting in the grandstand. Looking across the pitch I can still see where me and my father used to stand on the terraces and it never occurred to me that someday I'd be sitting over here. I wish that the players wouldn't charge around like that before the game even starts. Slow down lads. You'll use up all your energy and then where will we be?

15.35. The match is on and everybody knows the players by name because they are local lads. The stadium is buzzing with excitement and skill yet there are many empty spaces on the terraces because lots of people would rather stay at home and watch English soccer on their televisions.

15.40. I wish that we still played our international matches in Dalymount Park and women sold "Carberry's Chocolate" and little boys said "Hey mister, would ye lift us over the stile?" Those days are gone now and the team arrives at Lansdowne Road by bus because if they didn't they'd spend most of the afternoon wandering around Dublin trying to find the place. But I'm not going to say that because I'll only get into trouble.
*

Going For Gold

We can still get the Olympic Games for Dublin. But we need to hit the organisers with a bit of imagination and style. If we can sell them the notion of some thrilling new events we're as good as there. I can't help noticing that whenever I clip my toenails they whiz up into the air. Sometimes they shoot halfway across the room and I can't find them for ages. If I concentrate very hard I can get them to land in eggcups with little scores written on the side. There is the genesis of our first new Olympic event. The Toenail Clippiad. On a really good day I can send one of my big toenails spinning over as far as the beanbag. That's a distance of two and a half metres. I have measured it. With a following wind I could probably get one out through the letterbox. Last Tuesday I angled one up into the lightshade although it probably doesn't count because I was aiming at the coal scuttle. We can even have a Martial Arts section where two contestants sit facing each other in their bare feet. At a given signal they aim at their opponent and start clipping for all they're worth. Whoever scores the most direct hits inside one minute is the champion. They can both wear goggles if they wish. The Olympic Safety Committee would probably insist on it anyway.

Every Sunday in churches all over Ireland men and women cling onto the end bit of each row and defend it against all comers. You can try wriggling in against them and using your bottom as leverage. You can sit in their lap and drill into their ribcage with your elbow but you'd need a garden fork to shift them. This is a natural Olympic team event. We can call it a Dislodgiad and hold it in the Pro-Cathedral. The starting pistol can be fired by a Papal Nuncio.

It is crucial that we suggest a few events which we've got an odds-on chance of winning. If we can get a Begrudgiad into the Olympics we'll walk it.

Each competitor is given the name of a famous person either living or dead. Then they've got two minutes to do a wipe-out, character assassination job on them: '' His mother used to take in washing ... I knew him when he hadn't got an arse in his trousers...'' we could make this event our own.

Formation Posing and Shaping is another area where we would be well-nigh unbeatable. Each nation shall be invited to enter teams of young men with wispy virgin moustaches who shall lunge with their heads and shoulders, strut with their legs, spit between their teeth and ask the judges: '' What's the bleedin' story, pal?'' Toenails shall make this country great.

*

Scatter Me Round The Penalty Spot

I've decided to be cremated. When everybody rises up on the Last Day I don't want to be trampled in the rush. I think I'll be much safer if I'm sort of floating around on the edges of the stampede as a nice little cloud of ash.

I was making my will not so long ago but my solicitor advised me against the bit I wanted to add on at the end. My plan was to have all my relatives gathered together in his office. Before they arrive he spells out my last message on the wall behind the desk in invisible adhesive. After my will is read, the solicitor throws my ashes over his shoulder with a flourish and the following words appear as if my magic — "Don't forget to feed my cats!"

I would love my ashes to be scattered around the penalty area in Dalymount Park. I follow Bohemians and I like the notion of the lads going in for a cup of tea at half time with little bits of me on the bottom of their boots.

I was talking to an old woman on the bus and disclosed to her that I've decided upon cremation. She stared at my hearing-aid. "Make sure you take the batteries out of that yoke first," she warned. "Or they'll blow up and put the heart across everyone."

I don't know who sings *The Runaway Train* but that's one of the songs that I want. I've always loved it and all my friends can join in on the bits where the train goes "Whoooo!" I'd also like *The Laughing Policeman*, anything at all by *The Singing Dogs*, plus *I Know An Old Lady Who Swallowed A Fly*.

There are certain records which I would like to be put in with me. *Tie a Yellow Ribbon, Tulips from Amsterdam, The Hucklebuck* and the complete works of Max Bygraves. My friends will be invited to bring along their own pet-hate records and I'll be only too happy to take them with me as well.

I don't much care for the idea of being scattered around Dublin Bay or anywhere else in the Irish Sea for that matter. I wouldn't even dip my little toe into the water at Dollymount, so I've certainly got no desire to be dumped over the side of a rowing boat.

All things considered I'll settle for Dalymount Park but I don't want to go on the penalty spot. I'm allergic to that white stuff that they put on the pitch.

*

Small Obsessions, But Mine Own

I love standing underneath railway bridges. The one over Pearse Street is brilliant. The trains make a lovely rumble as they rattle into the station. I was standing there last week grooving to the rhythm of the wheels overhead. "Diddle dee dee ... diddle dee dee ... diddle dee dee." The last carriage off the bridge destroyed me. It only did a "diddle dee". The last "dee" was missing. Suddenly I felt incomplete. My biorhythms were upset. I was missing a dee. I waited under the bridge for the next couple of trains in the hopes that at least one of them would have an extra dee. No luck. So I walked around town for a while seeing how far I could get without stepping on a line. I was going great until a man barged into me in Dame Street. I was furious. "Now look what you made me do. Thanks to you I have to go back to the beginning of Westmoreland Street and start all over again."

I used to think that I was the only one who walks around town doing this sort of thing. Then I met a man in Bewleys who counts hairpieces. He said that he just can't help himself. He even sets targets. At the moment, according to his own code of rules he isn't allowed to go home until he has counted at least 20.

I knew a woman in Rialto who was convinced that there was a leak in every letterbox. It was a highly selective leak which only ever pitched her letter back out onto the pavement. Whenever she was posting a letter she first took off her coat, rolled up her sleeve and wedged her hand in as far as the elbow. That way she believed that she got the letter down beyond the leak.

Some people simply have to sit on an outside seat. They won't budge for anybody. Others have to be the one who presses the button which opens the door on the DART. If you get to it before them they go into a sulk which can last all day. When I bought myself a stopwatch last summer I became obsessed with timing things. After a week I knew the precise duration of my tummy rumbles, yawns, coughs, sneezes and other miscellaneous bodily eruptions. I followed an earwig all the way across the kitchen floor to get a time on him. I even worked out an average time for the nervous twitches in my left arm and the shudders from my fridge. I only ever worry about obsessions if they make me late for my tea

*

We're Lost Without The Mentals

I met a man last week who can't stop doing tots. He walks around Dublin all day long adding up columns of figures in his head. "It's the only thing I was good at in school," he said. "So I keep my brain ticking over in case somebody advertises a job for a Totter." We were standing beside each other at a bus stop when he suddenly spoke to me. "Nine thousand, six hundred and eighty pounds, and fifty pence," he said.

"But where would you get it?" I asked. He indicated the bus stop. "It's the total of all those bus times in pounds and pence," he replied. He said that he can give me the total of every list of bus times in Dublin city. "In Irish currency or Sterling," he added. He is very unhappy that there is nowhere for him to check his totals. "I think that Dublin Bus should put the right answer upside down on the back of each bus stop," he said.

He told me that he used to enjoy adding up the hurling scores on the radio and converting them into roods and perches. "But then the hurling went metric, so I had to give it up." He also told me in strict confidence about a medical condition called Mental Jellification. "I can even pinpoint the day it started," he said. "It was when they done away with the Primary Certificate Exam and 'The Mentals' in the schools." He said that 'The Mentals' kept young brains agile and active. "You had to add up these columns of figures in your head without using a pen or paper. Young brains never got the chance to jellify." Now they're all using calculators and the school children's brains are slowly setting like coloured jelly. Doctors tried to melt the jelly by sitting the youngsters underneath very hot hair dryers, but it merely ran into their memory banks and they even forgot their own names. " You never ever got wrong change in a shop until they done away with 'The Mentals'," he said. "If you brought home new curtains, they always fitted your windows, you were never one sock short after visiting the launderette, and you never had a button left over when you done up your waistcoat." This man has even offered to work voluntarily as an unpaid Totting Instructor. "I am prepared to bring groups of school children around Dublin from bus stop to bus stop adding up the times in their heads and converting them into Sterling." More than this a man cannot do.

*

Trying Not To Lose The Head About Things

I can even pinpoint where the fear first started. I was sharing the bill with a folksinger, a ventriloquist, two dancers and a man who guillotined teddy bears. I'm still not sure why exactly they wanted a poet, but you don't ask questions like that when you need the work. I used to stand in the wings and watch teddy bears' heads go flying in all directions. I'm not too sure why exactly the man wanted to do it, but there is an unspoken rule in showbusiness. You never question other artistes' professional integrity. So I never asked him about his guillotine. I used to stand there thinking: "My goodness, I would hate my head to go whizzing through the air like that." I honestly thought that I'd forgotten all about it.

I was sitting in a pub last week not worrying about anything. I wish that I hadn't looked up at the ceiling, because I saw this huge golden fan spinning around directly above me. Suddenly I got a flashback and my mind was filled with flashing blades and teddy bears.

The fan wasn't wobbling. I'll give it that much. Sometimes they spin and wobble at the same time, and that finishes me off completely. I called a waiter over. "Excuse me — I'm sure that your golden fan has been wind-tunnel-tested and everything, but just supposing it went spiralling through the air. Do you have any idea of its approximate range ?"

He said that nobody had ever asked him a question like that before. He said that people don't worry about things like that. So I explained to him about the guillotine and the teddies and asked him if he thought that the fan was capable of reaching the tables over in the corner. He said don't quote him on this or anything, but in his opinion it would most probably go straight out through the window. That was all I wanted to know. I moved over to the table furthest from the window and sat there not worrying about anything again.

Huge big concrete blocks worry me too. The ones that are wedged behind tall cranes which reach out over the pavement. I always walk on the far side of the street. I feel safer over there because the blocks aren't spinning or wobbling the way that the fans do. You don't have to work out the range or anything. I don't walk over gratings in the pavement because I'm afraid of suddenly wakening up in a pub cellar surrounded by barrels of beer. Apart from that I think I'm grand.

*

The More The Merrier

I've decided that there's safety in numbers. That is why I own ten front door keys. My sister has got one of them. So has my mother. I've lodged another in the bank for safekeeping. The other seven are floating around the house. The theory is great. Whenever I'm rushing out, I can always put my hand on at- least one of them in a hurry

The problem is that I start to feel insecure when I do a spot-check and can only account for three or four door keys. I fly into a panic. "Oh my God — the numbers are down. I'd better get a few more cut just to be on the safe side." So I come home with three new ones and then the missing ones turn up and for a couple of days I'm well into double figures.

A psychology book which I bought in Easons tells me that I'm suffering from an obsessive anxiety. As far as I'm concerned, I just want to make sure that I don't lock myself out of the house.

It has now started to spread into other areas of my life. There was a time when I felt perfectly relaxed with just the one toilet roll. Now I can't face the world with confidence unless there are at least twenty of them packed into the hotpress upstairs.

It's fierce. Sometimes I get this wild panic attack during which I race upstairs and fling the hotpress door open. Then I do a frenzied count and sink to my knees with relief. "Thanks be to God I've still got the twenty."

Friends sometimes express surprise when they come into my house. They are not used to seeing an infinite number of combs, nailfiles, boxes of paper hankies and disposable lighters lying around all over the place. Maybe it's perfectly healthy behaviour. Perhaps the book is wrong. I hate to waste time searching for things. Nonetheless I can't walk past somebody who is shouting "Four lighters for a pound" without feeling this crazy compulsion to bring home another twenty or so.

Perhaps I should have a preliminary chat with a psychologist. But they always ask you things about your family history. Then I'd have to talk about the coalhouse. When we were kids there were enough tins of dogfood stockpiled in there to feed 101 Dalmatians. Sometimes my father used to fling the door open and stand there with his lips silently moving. Then he'd relax and say " "Thanks be to God . . . one hundred and thirty five." I know exactly how he felt.

*

Aniseed Flashbacks

10am. Today was going to turn into one of the most glorious days of my life but I didn't know that yet.

10.15am. The glory started in my local bank. What sudden unexpected joy. One of the bank cashiers offered me an aniseed ball ... a real genuine authentic aniseed ball just like the ones I used to buy forty-odd years ago. It had the same taste and texture and everything. Then the cashier revealed to me the precise location of the sweet shop where I could buy myself as many aniseed balls as I wanted. I had just withdrawn £80 and was seriously tempted to blow the lot.

10.20am. My tongue had gone all red. I knew this for certain because I stopped a woman outside the bank and asked her: " Excuse me, madam-would you kindly have a look at my tongue and tell me what colour it is." Straight away she knew exactly what she was looking at. "My God, I don't believe it," she said. "You are actually eating an aniseed ball!" I whispered the address of the shop to her and she jumped up and down with excitement. Then she rushed into the bank to take out loads of money.

10.25am. I completely lost the run of myself in the sweetshop and bought two bags full. My hands were trembling. All the way home I was sticking out my tongue as far as it would go and forcing my eyes downwards so that I could see it for myself.

11am. After eating about thirty or so aniseed balls I started to get wild flashbacks. All of a sudden I was blurting out whole chants from my childhood.   In the middle of a telephone conversation with my mother I suddenly burst into "I made you look, I made you stare, I made the barber cut your hair. he cut it long, he cut it short, he cut it with a knife and fork."

Noon. A man came to my door with first-aid charts. He was selling them from house to house. Mid-way through his sales patter I heard a voice, which I recognised as my own, chanting "Cowardy cowardy custard, stick your nose in mustard!"   The poor man folded up his charts and departed without another word. I honestly don't blame him.

2pm. I had eaten about fifty aniseed balls by this stage and was completely out of control. My three cats went into deep shock at the sight of me sticking my head out of the bedroom window and yelling at the top of my voice "Up the airy mountain, down the rushy glen, we daren't go a hunting for fear of little men !"

2.30pm. I went to bed and stayed there for the rest of the day. Under the circumstances it was the safest place to be.

*

Where Does My Confidence Go?

Sometimes I skip up the stairs to bed singing "Hey Nonnie Nonnie No" and I feel great. I feel so great that I can't go to sleep so I lie there full of confidence singing "Climb Every Mountain" and "Champion the Wonder Horse"

If tomorrow came while I was still awake singing my songs I'd have no fears about facing into the new day. I'd surge out of bed and scatter my problems with the jawbone of an ass. No bother.

I think that my confidence creeps out very quietly while I am asleep and hides somewhere. I tried to isolate its exit point by putting cotton wool into all of my outlets. I blocked up my ears and my nostrils and everywhere else and went to sleep with a dentist's mask over my mouth.

The experiment was a partial success. When I woke up next morning my confidence was gone but I was able to cross off lots of possible escape routes on my check list.

I now believe that it leaves my body in the form of an invisible energy. It waits until I am sound asleep and then whispers — "OK, Let's go." I doubt very much whether it seeps downwards into the mattress because that would be much too easy.

In the morning you could wriggle in underneath it and whack the top of it with a sweeping brush. Your confidence would be so happy to get away from the bashing that it would charge back into you and say — "My goodness — I'm never going into that mattress again."

I think it's more likely that it rises upwards and goes out through the roof. At that precise moment you start to experience anxiety dreams about missing crucial trains and forgetting your lines on stage and suddenly finding yourself leading the community singing at Wembley Stadium with no clothes on.

Where exactly it goes to when it escapes through your roof and hits the night air is anybody's guess.

One of my own theories is that it attaches itself to bats. I think that you need a hell of a lot of confidence to whiz around in the dark like that without hitting anything. Perhaps it is our confidence that they are using. I'm not really sure.

All I know for certain is that I feel great last thing at night. Next morning I'm in bits. Perhaps we should take a close look at how bats feel when they are hanging upside down in their caves. This might give us the answer.

*

Open The Throttle And Turn Me Loose!

I'm going through one of my steam train periods at the moment. I always know when it's coming. Suddenly while I'm walking home up Vernon Avenue. I find myself making little steam engine noises. Gentle sounds like "Ch...Ch...Ch."

I used to do the whistle as well but I found that unexpected "Woo Woos" can make people leap off the pavement into the oncoming traffic. So I just do quiet little engine noises now and keep my "Woo Woos" to myself.

After a day or two of shunting myself up and down the stairs I start doing the sound of goods carriages banging into one another in a siding. It's a lovely satisfying "Plink plonk plink plonk plonk." If you keep it going long enough you go into a sort of transcendental state where absolutely nothing can bother you. I only ever plink plonk in the privacy of my own home.

A day later I need my cassette tape. I put it on and suddenly my whole house is resounding to the noise of steam engines shunting and slipping on icy tracks and hurtling through stations. A woman rang me up yesterday just as the Edinburgh to London express was thundering through York Station. "My God" she said "What's that?" So I told her.

" It's an A4 class Pacific locomotive number 60023 on its way up to Edinburgh." There was a long silence. The only sound was train wheels going clickedy click. Then she said something. "Oh....I see." People often say that to me on the phone.

Full credit to the doctors who helped me to cope with depression and anxiety. But I never told them about my steam train periods. I was afraid that they might clear them up. Sometimes I lay in bed in the hospital and the Reading to Guildford train was climbing up the summit between Gomshall and Chilworth. But I kept it to myself. I made my steam train noises into the pillow.   The last thing I wanted was special tablets which would take away my capacity for shunting and slipping on icy railway tracks.

I was talking to an old man recently and he said that he really misses the little black smuts that used to blow into your eye. '' Put your head out the window of a steam train and you could always depend on one of them smuts'' he said. ''Put your head out nowadays and you'd get a belt of a brick.''

''Woo Woo'' I said.

'' I wouldn't doubt you '' he replied.

*

Afraid To Get Up

10am: I'm still in my bed because I'm afraid to get out of it. It's one of those mornings when the fearful phantoms are on the prowl. They're swarming around the bed and blitzing me with catastrophic thoughts. ''Put even one little toe out from under the covers and the sky is going to fall on you.''

10.10am: My inspirational message on the wall isn't working anymore. ''Do That Which You Fear Most And The Death Of Fear is Assured.'' Perhaps I've read too many times and worn the message out. I'd love to meet the person who wrote it right now. ''Help! I'm stuck in this bed and that thought of yours isn't inspiring me anymore. Please think of something else, fast.'' On reflection, I think that all inspirational thoughts and cards should carry a ten year guarantee.

10.15am: I feel so safe in this duvet right now that the only thing capable of getting my feet on the floor is the theme music from *Jonathan Livingston Seagull* played very loud, Richard Burton's voice reading excerpts from *The Prophet* or a personal message from Superman.

10.20am: The Samaritans are doing sterling work and I salute them. But I believe that we need an emergency phone line for early morning tremblers who confidently expect the sky to come crashing down around their ears. You simply call them up and they coax you out of bed with lots of love and understanding.

10.25am: On the other hand perhaps it's possible to spend the rest of your life in bed. Maybe you can get little hover-jets fitted to the mattress and they whiz you around from place to place. You'd probably need a licence though, and they'd make you do a very hard test with emergency stops and hill starts.

10.45am: The guilt is the worst. The longer that I lie here, the worse I feel. Perhaps I should set fire to the mattress. A psychologist once told me that my bed is a womb-substitute. It's all very well for him to talk. The sky probably never whammed him squarely on the head.

11am: Blast it. There's someone at the front door and they won't go away. I'd better go down and have a look. Maybe my girl-friend has come back.

11.02: It's a man selling lines at one pound each, to help people who are suffering from head injuries. Honestly. That's exactly what he told me. I bought three. If the sky falls on me now, at least I'm adequately covered.

*

A Very Long Night

3.30am. I dread nights like these. It's over three hours since I went to bed and I'm still wide awake. It's not as if I'm worrying about anything. My mind isn't racing. I'm just lying here with the light on and I haven't got a clue what I'm going to do until breakfast time. I've already made a tent with the bedclothes and pretended that I'm in a circus. I've pulled feathers out of my pillow and puffed them up into the air. I've even made duck and hen shadows on the wall with my fingers. God — it's going to be a long night.

3.45am. If I was little and this was forty-odd years ago I could always start shouting — "Ma... I can't go asleep!" Then my mother would be awake and with any luck my brother would wake up beside me as well and I'd have somebody to talk to. But when you live on your own you just lie there and listen to the house making mysterious creepy noises. A dog barks somewhere and you start to think about graveyards and pale-faced women in wispy nighties who pretend to like you and then spoil everything by biting your neck.

3.50am. Funny. I'm four years in this house and I've never been up in the attic. I'm going downstairs to bring up the rocking chair because if I stand up on the wickery seats they'll collapse under my weight. I'm starting to feel excited about having a look under my roof. Maybe there are stuffed bears or treasure maps up there.

3.55am. This is more dangerous then I thought. Every time I lunge upwards with the sweeping brush, my rocking chair wobbles wildly. The last thing I want is to pitch headfirst down the stairs and land in the cats' litter tray. That is why I've wedged pillows under the rockers. Now it's steady enough for me to ease myself up onto the arms of the chair and grip on with my toes. There's no turning back now.

4.00am. A couple of good whacks with the brush and my attic is open. A sudden downward draught of cold air. Even though there is nobody else in the house I'm starting to feel a trifle self-conscious. I have never before perched up on the armrests of my rocking chair dressed in my underpants with a sweeping brush in my right hand. If anybody broke into my house now and saw me like this they would surely surrender to our Neighbourhood Watch and tell everyone.

4.05am. Onwards and upwards. I've got my elbows and upper half into the attic. The rest of me is down below kicking and waving my legs in the air. Wriggle, lunge, whoosh and suddenly I'm safe... high and dry in my own attic. God — it's dark up here. And very silent. There should be cheers and speeches of welcome and bands playing. There should be a phone so that I can ring somebody and tell them. Thank goodness the postman comes bright and early. I can tell him first. Roll on breakfast.

*

Father Mathew's Missing Bits

I think that somebody should fix the hole in Charles Stewart Parnell's trousers. I never really noticed it before. It's down near the bottom of his right leg. Normally I would have walked past his statue without a second glance. I am not in the habit of checking out the legs of famous people's pants. But I had just discovered that Father Matthew's fingers are gone. "My goodness," I said to a taxi driver. "Just look up there ◻. all of Father Matthew's fingers are gone. Do you think that a hungry bird pecked them off or what?" "He still has his thumbs all the same," he observed. "So the bird can't have been that hungry." It seemed only natural to check Charles Stewart's fingers after that because I was going down in that direction anyway. "Thank heavens," I said to another taxi driver. "Charles Stewart Parnell has got all his fingers."

"And his thumbs," he added . "Father Matthew hasn't," I said. "His thumbs?" he asked. 'No," I said. "His fingers." "You can't have everything," he replied. I don't know what manner of impulse prompted me to run my eye down the right leg of the trousers. And there it was. A little roundy hole. Big enough to let the rain or earwigs in. I don't expect Dublin Corporation to put up an expensive scaffolding or anything like that. There are far more pressing needs in the city than attending to a hole in Charles Stewart's trousers. But it wouldn't cost very much to stick a bit of chewing gum or Polyfilla into it and then cover it up with black paint. I would be more than happy to donate the chewing gum myself. I only ever chew the sugar-free variety but I'm sure that won't make any difference. One of Daniel O'Connell's angels could do with a bit of gum and a lick of paint while they're at it. I would urge the city fathers to check out our other urban streets because I'm afraid to look.

One leaky pair of pants and eight missing fingers is about as much as I can handle.

*

Jumpers, String And Rampant Hoot

10.30 am The man in the shop really does want me to buy the jumper. It is two sizes too big for me. "They're all wearing them like that," he says He doesn't realise that I'm going to buy it anyway. Jumpers always shrink after I buy them so I deliberately choose ones which are too big for me and then I shrink them down to my size. I've got a wardrobe full of jumpers just like the ones that my little sister used to put onto her dolls.

10.33 am: I'm standing here with the jumper on. The arms are flapping and hiding my hands and the rest of it nearly comes down to my knees. "Ah yes." said the man. "That's perfect grunge... men in our position need a bit of grunge."

10.35 am. "Will it shrink when I wash it?" I ask him. He shakes his head vigorously "Oh God, no," and he points at the label with lots of little symbols on it. People in shops are trained to tell you the garments won't shrink. They are not accustomed to shoppers who are resigned to taking clothes out of the wash two sizes smaller than when they went in. I buy the jumper anyway and boil it in a saucepan when I get home. It's a perfect fit now.

11 am: I'm harvesting string with a scissors in my sitting room. I'm still not sure whether it grows out of the carpet or what. I bought the carpet for £60 in a sale and it certainly wasn't advertised as a fertile string plantation. But long bits keep sticking out of it sideways and I cut them off and use them to tie up my binbags. After three bumper years of harvesting the carpet it still looks exactly the same size. Perhaps if I water it regularly I can double the crop.

11.25 am: Hoot arrives home from his active manoeuvres. He has been out on the Ho-Chi-Ming trail for the past six nights and, like all committed tomcats, he takes his duties very seriously. He wolfs down his breakfast and falls asleep standing up beside his dish.

1-1.35 am: After a close examination of Hoot I have 'concluded that non-stop sex with a multiplicity of partners whose names you don't know has the following side-effects: (a) It makes your whiskers lovely and springy; (b) your tail twitches while you're asleep; (c) it triples your appetite and gives you a brilliant deep throaty meow.

Mid-afternoon: I am finding it very difficult to concentrate on my writing because Hoot is now asleep on his back with his legs sticking straight up into the air and he keeps chattering his teeth together and vibrating his whiskers. Oh happy cat.

*

One At A Time Please

I like it when one person visits me in my house. I ask them if they'd like tea or coffee and they tell me and I race out to the kitchen concentrating very hard on their answer. I repeat it over and over again in my head. "White coffee with two sugars... white coffee with two sugars." That is as much as my mind can handle at one time. If the person then starts shouting questions out to me about soccer or Jaffa cakes or ear-piercing, I am able to answer them as if they are getting my full attention but my mind is still concentrating like mad on their milk and sugar.

If more than one person arrives I find it necessary to explain my position very distinctly. "In a couple of seconds I am going to ask you if you'd like tea or coffee. I would appreciate it if the first person speaks slowly and clearly and says it just once. Then I would like the second person to repeat what the first person has said before adding on their own bit. Then when everybody has completed the joined-up statement I would like us all to sit here for about five minutes chanting it together until I know it off by heart. Then and only then will I go out to the kitchen. Thank you."

I don't have the faintest idea how bar persons cope. I would have no difficulty working behind a bar if everybody in the whole world drank a glass of fizzy orange and nothing else. No bags of crisps or peanuts or change for the cigarette machine or any other fiddly bits like that. Sometimes I'm in a crowded pub and the noise level is fantastic and the patrons are two and three deep at the counter and everybody is shouting out long complicated orders. The bar person doesn't start to tremble or cry or hide down behind the counter calling for his Mammy. Some of them are able to talk at the same time and they give you the right change and everything. I admire bar staff more than astronauts or brain surgeons or university lecturers. I think that we should show videos of them in action to all our secondary school students.

I can't remember other peoples' names either. I think it would be lovely if we all had them tattooed onto our foreheads. You could relax straight away into a new group of people. It would also help if each person in the group repeated their name out loud once every fifteen seconds. You could keep this going for the first half hour or so.

I also can't remember whether I put my right or my left leg into my jeans first, but that is a different thing entirely.

*

Half and Half

Funny. I must have crossed Capel Street Bridge millions of times. But I only noticed them for the first time today. Lots of half-horse, half-fish sort of creatures. Painted green. The top half is a perfectly formed horse. It looks so real that I said "Giddy up" to it.

The bottom half is a lovely plump fish's body. The whole thing came as quite a surprise. I can take a half-man, half-horse in my stride. I've seen oodles of them. Those lads are called centaurs and you wouldn't cross the street to look at one of them. But the horse and fish combination is a new one on me. I have never come across that particular dynamic before.

I suppose you'd call them merhorses or whinnyherrings. You would probably feed the top half with hay and keep the lower section immersed in a barrel full of salty water. I'm not really sure.

What saddened me a little was the use to which the bridge builders have put these fabulous mythological creatures. They are holding up lamp standards with their heads. Here is a creature who is both capable of winning the Grand National and swimming the Irish Sea before breakfast. I think it deserves better.

There is a noble unicorn sitting up on top of the Custom House. He has been given a bit of dignity. Himself and a lion are minding a coat of arms so that nobody nips onto the roof on the way home from an all-night party and robs it. I think that the horsey fishes should be doing something like that.

With a modicum of imagination we could put up some brand new city statues which would be the talk of the civilised world. Why stop at equine fishes? How about putting up a few half-cat, half-mouse figures along the parapet of O'Connell Bridge. The top half could be chasing the bottom bit around in circles and never catching it.

I have never seen a half-man, half-lawnmower but I have no trouble imagining one. We could put loads of them into Fairview Park and they could spend their time going backwards and cutting the grass.

I love Jersey cows. 1 particularly like their subtle use of the eye-liner and their sweeping lashes. I am also mad about soccer. Perhaps the City Fathers can erect a half-Jersey cow, half-central defender outside Dalymount Park. The top half can moo at the rising sun and the bottom section shall take crucial penalty kicks. I will be more than happy to model the bottom bit if somebody will loan me a pair of football boots.
*

Meandering Around With A Bag Of Bananas

11.30am: I told the woman that I bring the bananas to bed with me. She said you could do a lot worse and sold me ten for a pound. I told her that whenever I waken from a bad dream during the night I usually eat two or three and then go back to sleep. But my figures never balance in the morning. There are always a lot more banana skins than that around the bed. A helpful little man beside her suggested that I possibly eat some in my sleep as well. He suggested that I buy an abacus so that I could keep an accurate record for myself.

11.40am: I wandered into the Pound Shop in O'Connell Street to buy an abacus and got a lovely kaleidoscope instead.

11.45am: I was sitting under a statue munching one of my bananas and watching three inner-city crows building their nests within cawing distance of The GPO. An old man sat down beside me and said "Where would you be without the trams?" He sounded very sad about it so I gave him a banana and a go with my kaleidoscope.

11.50am: The old man said that he had a huge problem with film stars and television celebrities. He saw a TV weatherman in the street last week and wanted to ask him if he ever got nervous in front of the cameras. "But I always lose my nerve. Then I sort of follow them trying to get my courage up and I do be ducking into doorways and bending down behind cars so they won't see me. Then I do be worried in case they think that I'm stalking them."

Noon: I crossed the street to say hello to Austin who sells newspapers and books outside the Irish Permanent. He also puts up posters for my poetry gigs, so the very least I owed him was a banana.

12.30pm: I didn't mean to start crying in the ILAC library. But three or four men were sitting in front of a television with orange headphones on their ears. They were watching a video of Manchester United and Benfica in the European Cup Final.

Suddenly the match was over and each of the players was embracing Sir Matt Busby in turn and some of them were crying with emotion. I stood there thinking about the Munich air disaster and old men and trams and I had to go and hide behind the bookshelves because wet tears were running down my face and plopping onto the carpet.

11.45pm: I bought a packet of football candy sticks to try and get a picture of Paul McGrath but got some guy I never heard of who plays for Chelsea instead. The man in the shop wouldn't let me look in the packet before I bought it, which I though was the pits. So he got neither a go with my kaleidoscope nor a free banana. If anybody has got a candy stick photo of Paul McGrath I've got millions of swaps.

*

Get Me Out Of Here!

The only time I feel fully relaxed at a party is when I'm in the bathroom. I close the door behind me and all of a sudden the pressure is off. I don't have to look like I'm having a great time or anything. I don't have to talk and laugh and say intelligent things. Sometimes I feel like staying in there all night.

People are standing around outside holding a glass in one hand and a plate in the other. It is impossible to scratch your nose if it gets itchy. Little groups are beginning to form and nobody wants to be left standing on their own.

This is the stage when I start to panic. Please grant that I finish up as part of a group. Please don't let me finish up standing on my own. People will think that there's something the matter with me. It's just like when a ship is sinking and everybody wants to be in a lifeboat.

It's amazing how much punishment that you'll put up with. People will talk to you on subjects which are so boring that they could take the paint off a door. You'll stand there and nod and look utterly engrossed because you know that the hostess is watching.

All of a sudden food doesn't look like itself anymore. Nobody likes to ask what anything is because you're supposed to know. Little strips of meat or fish or something are criss-crossed on top of thick liquidy stuff which is plastered onto a cracker. Take one bite and the whole thing comes apart in your hand.

After about three hours or so, people will begin to feel the strain of laughing at everything that other people are saying. An uneasy silence grips the room. This is the time to head for the toilet and barricade yourself in.

Sooner or later some malcontent is going to suggest "a bit of a song" and an icy hand grips each and every stomach. Someone is going to be asked and suddenly everybody is staring at the floor.

The party has now become an exercise in survival. Nobody wants to sing, so everybody in the room is yelling someone else's name.

Guests are picking on one another with a frightening intensity because the best form of defence is attack. This exercise in ritual humiliation is known as "The Sing-Song."

Whatever became of Blindman's Buff, Pinning The-Tail-On-The-Donkey and lovely red jelly?

*

Christy's On The Roof

8.30 a.m.— Woke up on the sitting room floor... cold, stiff as a starched shirt and slumped back against the beanbag. The last thing I could remember was listening to my relaxation tape at midnight. It works.

They arrived together before breakfast. They even lay side by side on the mat I swear that an Bord Telecom and the ESB work closely as a team. "Let's wham Pat with a couple of good hefty bills today." I placed them out of sight into Pussy Willow's basket and he promptly fell asleep on top of them. Perhaps if I smear the envelopes with Tuna Whiskas he might even eat them for me.

9.10 a.m.— My phone rang during breakfast. Not only was it a wrong number but straight away a very bossy woman demanded that I get Christy. I told her a terrible lie. I said that he is still cowering up on the roof while a trained team of therapists are trying to coax him down with dishes of rice crispies and honey. She won't ring this number again.

10.00 a.m. — I can never fully get used to the idea of not actually going anywhere to work. Today I felt a little bit guilty about putting on a Chuck Berry tape, making a mug of coffee, taking the cover off my typewriter and saying: "all right, fingers ... Let's go... two bills in the post this morning so full steam ahead!"

11.30 a.m. — I was feeling great. I had made a good start into a brand new radio play about a man who programmes his remote control to make the toll-bridge go up and down whenever he feels like it. He also makes traffic lights change colour and stands at the Merrion Gates slowing down the DART.

12.00 midday — It's amazing the thoughts that suddenly hit you while you're fully immersed in a new radio play. "Ahhhhhh! Today is bin-day and I've completely forgotten to put out the plastic bags!" I forgot them last week as well. By this stage they were fermenting exotic gasses which bathed the yard with a luminous glow after dark. I was afraid to tie them shut in case they blew up and smashed every window in North Dublin.

12.0-13.00 hours — Had my lunch. Banana sandwiches and coffee. Thrilled the three cats with a brand new flavour. God, when I think of it — there's Blackie, Willow and Hoot banqueting on Chicken & Rabbit while their master munches on banana. There's gonna be a few changes made around here.

14.00 hours — A quick browse through my diary. It's almost time to start sending off posters for my poetry gigs in Meath,

Kilkenny and Galway. Still in two minds about which I enjoy most writing my poems or performing them. Somebody told me in Cork last week that I look like Albert Einstein on the posters. I hope nobody shows up at my gigs expecting to see him.

*

Mother Threw Out A Lemonade Lake

I hate the bit that you can't get at. When we were small, our mother used to buy huge bottles of lemonade with a siphon in them. You pressed the siphon down and the fizzy stuff rushed out and it was all bubbly and brilliant. But there was always a little bit of lemonade at the bottom which the siphon couldn't reach. That was the little bit that used to come between us and our rest. We used to shake the bottle and waggle it sideways but we were wasting our time. Sometimes we'd sit beside the bottle for hours and just look at it. Then the bottle would be thrown out and we'd break our hearts watching it being taken away in the bin-lorry. We'd lie in bed at night agonising about that little bit of lemonade going to waste in a rubbish dump somewhere. I figure that over the years my mother was responsible for throwing out the makings of a lovely big lemonade lake.

Aerosol cans are worse. I know that there is still a bit of underarm deodorant inside because I can hear it when — I shake the can up and down. I've tried pressing the squirter and muttering, "Come on out — I know you're in there." The can just responds with an empty splutter. Sometimes I stand them upside down overnight. I do the same with my bottles of bubble bath stuff. I curl my toothpaste tubes up from the bottom and then belt them with a hammer on the floor. If you wander into my bathroom, you'll see an infinite number of bottles and cans all standing on their heads.

There is usually a warning printed on aerosol cans. "Do not attempt to pierce this container or you will blow up your bathroom and you will never be seen again, although they may find bits of you in the next parish." I don't think that's very fair. How else are you supposed to get your hands on the shaving foam that refuses to come out? There is one thing I very much wish to say to the people who are responsible for putting toilet rolls together. "Will you kindly refrain from putting that gluey stuff at the beginning of the roll because I usually rip about two or three layers of tissue to bits before I get the thing up and running?" Sometimes — I see this little puppy on the television careering around somebody's house with a toilet-roll streaming along behind him. I'd love to give him one of my rolls with the gluey stuff at the start and say, "Right. If you're so smart, gallop round the house with that." Then he'd know all about it.

*

Do You Remember?

* Bringing home a loaf of bread which was still warm and picking a lump out of it with your finger. Then handing the loaf to your mother and making sure that the side with the big hole in it was facing away from her. * Warning your brother to keep his feet to himself and not to dare cross the invisible line which ran down the middle of the bed. * Feeling scared if you were still awake when you heard your parents turning off their bedroom light because if you were still awake when they fell asleep, the Bogey Man would surely get you. * Trying not to laugh during the family rosary.

* Wondering how long it was going to take you to grow into the new coat which came down as far as your shoes. * Watching your mother sitting beside a mountain of socks and patiently drawing a needle and thread in and out, in and out, until one by one the holes in the heels disappeared. * Racing round and round the cinema during the "talking" and "kissing" bits of the film, and suddenly sitting down again the moment drums started to beat, horses galloped or the barman in the saloon took down the mirror. * Watching big lumps of your hair falling

onto the floor of the barber's shop and thinking that he was never going to stop. When you went outside the back of your neck was freezing and little tickly bits of hair were in under the collar of your shirt. * Dredging black sludge up out of the inkwell at school with the nib of your pen. * Trying to pull your braces up over your shoulders and losing your grip so that they suddenly twanged back again. * The excitement in your tummy when you spotted a new circus poster pasted onto a brick wall. * The cold feeling when your father called up the stairs, "Come down here this minute — I want to talk to you." * Trying to get changed for a swim on the beach while keeping a towel wrapped around you, and wriggling out of your trousers and into your togs without letting anybody see anything. * Jelly for dessert on Sunday but you had to eat everything else first. * Not understanding any of the jokes that the other boys were telling about things which were bold, but laughing anyway so that nobody would know that you didn't know. * The sinking feeling in your tummy when two teams were being picked for a game of football on the road and even when you were the only person left they still didn't pick you, but one team said to the other, "And you can have him."
*

Confessions Of An Impulsive Man

The girl told me that she still finds it very difficult. She used to work as a hairdresser. Then she gave it up three years ago. Even now when she is sitting behind somebody on the bus she feels this powerful urge to grab a hold of their hair and start twirling it. It's ten times worse if she is behind a bald man. Then she gets this wild impulse to massage his scalp with her fingertips until it tingles with good health. That's why she always goes upstairs and sits at the very front.

I told her that sometimes I am walking along the pavement and I see a man bending forward over an open grating outside a pub. He is lowering down a barrel. I get this fierce urge to nudge him with my bottom as I walk past. It is an irresponsible urge and I am deeply ashamed of it. It's not like me at all.   I remember kneeling in a confession box years ago. I could hear lots of whispering going on behind the slide. Every so often the priest's voice would shoot up by about six octaves and you were simply dying to know what was going on. Then a third little voice appeared from nowhere and started to whisper in your ear. It was a brimstone scented voice with twin horns and a pointed tail. "Go on...have a listen ... put your ear up against the slide ... you never know what you'll hear." Suddenly a fourth voice joined in. "If that slide is suddenly whipped back and he catches you like that you'll be excommunicated on the spot." So I knelt there and systematically shoved my earlobes in and out with my fingers. That way the sound was distorted and I couldn't hear a thing.

I don't know where these urges come from. A friend of mine finds silence utterly unnerving. He always feels that it is pleading with him to break it with a song or a wild whoop. He has had to give up going into churches, public libraries, museums or the National Concert Hall.

I was sitting beside him during a Mahler symphony when he urgently whispered that the silence was begging him to start making foghorn noises at the top of this voice. It was grand until he mentioned it. There wasn't a bother on me. Suddenly we both had to leave in a hurry because once he told me, I could feel it too.

That's the whole trouble with those kind of urges. You catch them off people.

*

Fixations With Minkys And Bayonet Scars

I bought sixteen needles yesterday because a button came off my coat. I told the girl in the shop that I really only needed the one and approximately sixteen inches of black thread. She was very good about it. She didn't burst out laughing or anything.

She said that once upon a time her grandmother used to buy loose tea and a Woodbine and a match. But it's all packets now. So I've got fifteen needles that I don't want. I met a taximan on the way home who has got ninety-nine dowels. He said they're all over the house. He only wanted the one as well. I didn't feel so bad then.

I wanted to buy a pair of laces for my desert boots. "''What colour are they?'' asked the girl in the shop. "Are they minky?'' That is exactly the same way that Peter Sellers says "Monkey'' in the Inspector Clouseau films. I honestly thought that's what she meant. '' Monkey?'' I said. She shook her head firmly. '''No.'' she replied. "Minky.'' We repeated these words to one another four or five time before she asked me why I kept talking to her in a shoe shop about monkeys. I explained about Clouseau. I asked her why she had a fixation with minkeys She said she meant mink coats. There must be easier ways of buying a pair of laces.

I wanted to buy a pair of Jeans. It was my very first time in a communal changing room. The young guy beside me kept looking at my leg. '' I hope you don't mind me saying this Pat, but that's some scar you've got there.'' I told him the honest truth. I fell off a quayside in Scotland into the hold of a trawler full of live prawns.

The man beside us was also in his Y-fronts and bare legs. '' Where would you leave this one?'' he demanded, thrusting his left leg forward. We both inspected it. "Me and my brother were sword fencing with two old bayonets when we were kids,'' he said.

We both agreed that his scar was infinitely better than mine. The man was thrilled with himself.

The young guy seemed to think it was time he showed us something. So he displayed the stud marks on the back of his leg from last week's match. A man who had just come in with a new pair of trousers whipped up his shorts and showed us his appendix scar. We were all unanimous. It was a beauty.

Do women show one another things in communal changing rooms. If so — what? Until the mixed changing room comes along we shall probably never know.

*

Psssssst!

It's not big stresses that get to me. It's a whole combination of little niggly ones that are taking years off my life. It's the voices in my head that go to war whenever I'm nearing the "Pick 'N' Mix" in the supermarket. "Go on ...quick ... nobody's looking. Just roll past very casually and grab one of those pink marshmallows-they're lovely." "Don't be such a fool. There's probably an invisible beam across the front of the marshmallow section. Put your hand in there and alarm bells will start to ring and blue lights will flash and you'll be disgraced." "Rubbish-nobody cares about a little marshmallow. Think of all the money you're spending in here. At the very most, it's only a venial sin ...you don't go anywhere near Hell for them." "Hold it right there. Supposing they're got all these television screens up in the office with trained observers watching them. Put your hand near those sweets and a spotlight will pick you out. Then a metallic voice will boom, 'THAT PETTY CRIMINAL IS AFTER SWIPING A PINK MARSHMALLOW!'" I can't handle stress like that. I did pinch a sweet once and found it impossible to relax until I had swallowed the evidence. I was wheeling my trolley around the supermarket with a feeling of pink guilt in my mouth.

I don't know where these svoices come from. Sometimes I'm appearing on live television and my composure is wrecked by a tiny nagging whisper inside my head. "Hey you — yes, you Mr Cool. I'm not saying for one moment that it is, but supposing your fly is open right now!" Your immediate impulse is to whip your hand down for a quick spot check but you can't do things like that with over one million people watching your every move. I can handle the "Open Fly" voice when I'm posing my way down Grafton street, because you can always nip into a shop doorway, but there is nowhere to hide in front of three cameras.

Sometimes I'm sitting on a bus and I see somebody I know strolling along the pavement. We both wave to one another and the bus moves on. Suddenly the bus stops at traffic lights and you can sense the person catching up and you think, "Oh God, now I've got to wave again." So you both do a second self-conscious kind of wave and the bus moves on again. Now you're stuck in traffic again and thinking, "Oh no ...I just couldn't face a third one ...come on bus ... move ... here he comes again." I want a few huge big major chronic stresses. It's little ones like those that have me wrecked.

*

Guts For Garters

I cut my finger this morning. Back in the days when I used to exaggerate things it would have poured blood. There would have been blood splashing all over the kitchen floor. It would have taken an emergency tourniquet to stem the flow. But it didn't. My finger just bled a bit.

I now know what a disaster is. Pompeii. There was one. The Titanic. That was another. It is not a disaster if we fail to qualify for the European Soccer Finals. "My God-that was catastrophic last night." So I asked the man if a major war had broken out or what? "No," he said. "Bohemians lost 2-1."

It is as simple as getting a sense of proportion about things. It is very annoying to lose your front door key. It is extremely irritating when you can't find your bus ticket. But try to bear in mind that Bo-Peep mislaid an entire flock of sheep. The British lost an empire. During the French Revolution lots of aristocrats lost their heads. Now there is something to really put you off your dinner.

I think it would be truly miraculous is somebody clicked their fingers, muttered the word "Bizembee" and the Custom House disappeared. It would be even more miraculous if they said the word again and Ray Charles appeared in its place seated at a piano singing "Hit The Road Jack" Miracle' washing powders no longer impress me. Perhaps if they changed all my clothes into Louis Copeland suits, they might.

I have great difficulty in regarding any public performance by Frank Sinatra as 'The Ultimate Event'. If he parted the Red Sea while singing 'Songs For Swinging Lovers' we might be getting somewhere near it.   I have no desire to buy myself the 'Ultimate' vacuum cleaner unless it is one which knows intuitively when the house needs to be done. Then it plugs itself in and glides silently around the place until the job has been done to perfection.   Then it empties itself, puts the bags out for the binmen and leaves me a note to that effect before putting itself away again. That is ultimate.

A woman told me yesterday that she nearly died when she saw the state of her daughter's bedroom. She said that she is going to kill her when she sees her tonight. Her husband is going to murder their son because of his school report. He is going to have his guts for garters.   Vlad the Impaler used to talk like that. But I think he really meant it.

*

All Hail To Armitage Shanks

I would love to know who Armitage Shanks is. I desperately want to thank him. His name has been an integral part of so many of my wee-wees that I have lost count. I have seen it written on urinals from public bars to Grade A hotels. In fact. wherever two or three men are gathered together to do a wee-wee, there you will find Armitage Shanks.

I want to write a heartfelt letter of thanks to him. I feel as if I know him personally because we have shared so many private moments together. I feel deeply emotional whenever I think about it. "Dear Armitage, my name is Pat and I am nearly 51 years of age. Based on an average daily output of five wee-wees, I estimate that so far in my life I have done approximately 93,135. I have included an extra 60 in that figure to cover leap years. Armitage, I find this total absolutely awe-inspiring. I am not boasting or anything like that. Rather am I mindful of what a significant part you have played in my life. Thank you. And please thank Mrs. Shanks as well. If I ever reach the golden figure of 100,000 I hope to have some kind of a celebration and would love to invite yourself and your wife and all the little Shankses. I do hope that you can all come along. Yours with deep gratitude, Pat Ingoldsby." But I don't know where he lives in fact I don't know a solitary thing about him. I imagine that he leads the life of a county squire somewhere in Berkshire. His great-grandfather invented the urinal during a lengthy spell as a castaway on a desert island. One day while idly sketching in the white sand with a stick he suddenly said: "Gad, methinks I have stumbled upon something which will change the history of wee-wees as we know them." Which indeed he had. I imagine that the present day Armitage has got a very tasteful swimming pool which is shaped like a giant pink urinal.

This is not done out of a sense of ostentation but rather to honour the memory of his great-grandfather who staggered ashore at Dover after an epic swim home from his exile on a coral reef. Moments before he collapsed from exhaustion he sketched his blueprint in the English sand and signed it with another stick. The rest is social history.

Armitage, we'd be lost without you.

*

Spending A Penny Can Get Complicated

The man told me that he was just going off to the little boys' room. I had to think for a second. We were having a coffee in

Bewleys. Surely to God they haven't got a kiddies' playroom in there. "You're going where?" He thought for a second. "Eh — I'm just going to wash my hands." All of a sudden the monster in me took over. I decided to make this man actually say the word. "But your hands are perfectly clean. There's not a speck on them. In fact, seldom have I seen such a spotless pair." "No, no ... what I mean is ... I'm just going to see a man about a dog." The hell he was. You don't see dogs in restaurants. You most certainly don't do deals with men in coffee shops and actually buy one.

One of my aunties calls it the loo. I found myself wondering whether this man in Bewleys had got that particular word in his list of euphemisms. "Eh — you were saying something about dogs. Is it a red setter or what?" He was clearly bursting to go at this stage. "No-I don't mean real dogs. A visit. I'm going to pay a visit."

I told him that I love visits. Especially when the person that you're visiting has got a dog. You can bring it out for walks and throw sticks and shout "Fetch" and "Sit" and "Stay !"

The man was running out of time and polite expressions. So I decided to help him along a bit. "In all probability, what you really wish to tell me is that there is a tide in the affairs of men. William Shakespeare said that. The immortal bard recommended taking such a tide at the flood." I really shouldn't have said it. It seemed to have the same effect on him as when the nurses turn on all the taps in the ward to motivate a very shy patient. He simply couldn't wait any longer. He blurted out something about making his peace with nature.

"Ah — now you're talking! Wasn't it W.B. Yeats himself who used to lie on his couch in vacant and pensive, mood thinking about daffodils and sprightly dances?"

The man was in agony. He begged me to stop talking to him about poets and dogs. But he started it and now I just couldn't stop myself.

"Wasn't it William Masefield who wrote that it's a wild call and a clear call which may not be denied?" There was no response. The man was gone. To spend a fifty pence piece or a penny or something.

*

Kindly Keep To Your Half Of The Table

I love the dramatic change that takes place. One minute I'm walking down the street, not really owning anything big at all. Next minute I'm sitting inside a restaurant and suddenly, a table and four chairs are all mine. I haven't paid anybody a penny yet but everybody in the place knows the rules. "Excuse me sir, do you mind if I borrow one of your chairs?" That's what the man says. He knows. All of a sudden I want to ring up everybody I know who ever told me that I wouldn't make it. "Get yourself over here fast. Right now, I am in full command of an ashtray, a jug full of milk, a pink flower, a little bit of plastic with the number five on it, a white table cloth, four big chairs and a huge table. Yippee!"

What I can't stand is when the waiter lets me get settled in. He lets me get used to loaning out my ashtray and giving people little sups of milk out of my jug. I'm just beginning to get a lovely buzz out of giving chairs away when he says it. "I'm terribly sorry, but we're really busy here tonight-would you mind very much if I sit somebody else at your table?"

I feel like asking him, "How could you do a thing like this to me? How could you ask me to share my lovely pink flower with a complete stranger?" But I don't. I nod and the other person sits down. I feel like saying to them, "OK, you might be sitting here but this is my bit of plastic with the number five on it and that is my jug of milk and don't you start moving my flower around because I like it where it is. Oh, and stay over in your half of the table. My half starts from the ashtray so don't you go putting any of your things over on my side."

Some people are grand. They stay over in their own half and everything is fine. I wish that everybody was like that. I feel like a shot has been fired across my bow when somebody lights up and moves the ashtray deep into their territory. They don't ask you or anything. When they have finished their soup, they shove their empty dish over into your half. My brother was like that. We had an invisible line down the middle of our bed but he completely ignored it. He stuck his feet over into my half and sometimes other bits of him followed. They were all freezing cold.

A table for one isn't really the answer because I love owning lots of chairs as well. Maybe you're better off eating at home. I'm not really sure.

*

Please Have This One On Me

Pubs aren't too keen on the idea. They don't like to see people walking in off the street, making a bee-line for the toilets and then walking straight out again. They put notices up. "These toilets are for the use of our patrons only." That's why I always buy something first. A box of matches. Then I can do my wee-wee in comfort. If I've got someone with me and I'm treating them to a wee-wee as well, I cover them by buying a bag of crisps. "Have this one on me." Barmen seem to know. They catch your eye as soon as you walk in. "I know exactly what you're up to. You're one of those hit-and-run merchants. If you'd any sense of decency at all you'd buy a pint." You feel like a kid caught in an orchard with apples up his jersey.

I keep a list of pubs which owe me one. A notebook full of names of places where I've had coffee and sandwiches and not used their Gents during my visit. That way I build up lots of credit for myself. There are at least ten pubs in Dublin at the moment where I can walk in with a clear conscience, relieve myself and walk straight out again. I think that pubs should keep a similar list. That way the barman will know when to glower at you and when to smile. "Go ahead. You're OK, you had a ham sandwich in here on the 25th of October, 1990."

There's no problem whatsoever if you've got a child with you. You can rush in and everybody knows it's an emergency and people get out of your way in a hurry and men shout "Mind the child." The barman even holds the door open for you. You don't have to buy a box of matches or anything.

Posh hotels are great. You walk into the foyer and look around as if you're trying to find Lord and Lady Ponsonby-Smyth. What you're actually doing is trying to find the Gents sign. If your need isn't pressingly urgent you can even sit down for a while and have a free read. Lots of hotels keep the daily papers with a plank of wood attached so you won't go home with them. They're actually working against themselves because it's so much easier to light the fire with them when there's kindling wood attached. When it becomes obvious to all and sundry that the Ponsonby-Smyths aren't going to show up you simply do what you have to do and take to the hills.

If only we had decent civilised public conveniences, I'd save a fortune on matches and crisps.

*

Choosing A Book Can Be A Pain In The Neck

The doctors got it completely wrong. I hadn't been sleeping in a draught. I never do. The windows are all tightly closed in my bedroom to stop huge furry moths from coming in and biting my neck while I'm asleep. The alternative healer got it wrong too. She said that the pain at the base of my neck was actually unexpressed anger. She told me that I needed to whack cushions with a tennis racquet and shout at the top of my voice — "Take that you very naughty person!" But I boot a bean bag around the house about six times a week any way and call it far worse things than that.

An old man at the bus stop got it right. "Did you join a library recently?" he asked me. It was like one of those obscure questions that Hercule Poirot asks murder suspects. "Tell me my leetle fellow — when is the last time you visited the elephant house in Chester Zoo?" "There ye are then," said the old man. "There's your answer. You got your library ticket last week and then the neck started to play up." He said that it's the way they have the books on the shelves. All the titles are written sideways on the spines and you have to keep twisting your head to read them. "The whole thing is against nature."

" I'll tell you something else," he said. "The sister had to stop buying operatic cassette tapes for the same reason. She'd be down the library in the morning destroying her neck twisting her head this way and that. Then she'd go and compound the damage in the record shop reading the titles sideways on the Pavarotti tapes." He said she had to go to Lourdes with her neck and she hasn't borrowed a book or bought a tape since.

There has to he a better way. We have invented weighing scales which can tell the difference between a banana and a Brussels sprout. We can lower tiny cameras down peoples' throats and get candid shots of their follicles. It should not be necessary for consenting adults to walk around libraries and bookshops looking like whiplash victims.

An electric trolley may well be the answer. You lie on it sideways and rest your head on a cushion. Then you glide up and down the aisles effortlessly reading the titles. If the library service is stretched for money I have no objection to lying on a cheaper version which can be pushed by a trained operative. A periscope can be used to scan the top shelves. The Book Of Kells is lying down nice and flat. It never damaged anybody's health.

*

Bring Back The Album

All the albums are gone. I turned my back for a second and while I wasn't looking, somebody made them obsolete. "I'm sorry sir- we can only give it to you on cassette or CD." I don't want a cassette or CD. I want a lovely, big long-playing double album with colour photographs in the middle of Eric Clapton sitting beside palm trees.

Cassette tapes and CDs are much too small. You can't take them out of the bag on the bus and look at smashing centre fold spreads of Thin Lizzy doing the Live And Dangerous tour with smoke and coloured lights and roaring crowds. It was a great way of showing off what you had just bought. You were pretending to be checking out the pictures on the album and you were really announcing — "Look at me. I'm super-cool-look what I just bought." I want a free book as well. I got a fabulous one with The Beatles album *Let It Be*. I still read it. I want sleeve notes written by people who were obviously wired to the moon while writing them. I still don't understand a word on the early Rolling Stones albums. I love reading them. People used to say — "Do you mind if I look through your records?" Then they sat on the floor and tried to name all the people on the Sergeant Pepper cover. You'd be so busy opening up album covers and reading the sleeve notes that you wouldn't actually play a record for hours.

I want a free magnifying glass with my next cassette tape. The small print is tinier than the special offers you get on the back of matchboxes. I bought a Queen tape and the photographs of Freddy Mercury are smaller than a 32p stamp. I want the name and address of the person who decided that nobody needs albums anymore. I want to write to that person and tell them that I don't like feeling obsolete. While I'm at it I also want the name and address of the person who decided to remove the '78' speed from record players. I used to love watching the turntable whizzing around. I used to line up all my little Subbuteo men around the edges and then switch it on. Mark my words. Books will be next. We'll all be going home with little microfilms instead and then where will we be? You can't stand the teapot on a microfilm.

*

Gone For Good

I don't lend books or records any more. It's much too hard to get them back. I wish there was a professional snatch-squad listed in the Golden Pages. You simply give them the titles of the books and the addresses of the borrowers. You speak into the phone in a breathy whisper, "Do whatever you have to do — just get them back."

We're too polite. We don't like to upset people. We'd love to say something like, "Listen, you've had that book of mine long enough now to translate it into rhyming Sanskrit. I want it back and I want it back now."

We say other things instead. "Eh ...that book of mine ... no ... no ... I'm not rushing you or anything. I mean take your time ... whenever you do get around to finishing it, not a second before. Me? Want it back? God, whatever gave you that idea?"

Subtlety works brilliantly if you've got the nerve. "My eldest son ... the psychopathic kickboxer with the personality disorder ... he keeps asking me for your address. But I told him. 'Cool it son. You know how Mammy worries when you work yourself into a frenzy over poor Daddy's books. I'm sure that nice man will drop them back before the full moon tonight.' "

One friend of mine used to borrow records in bulk. "I'll just take all your Van Morrison, two or three box sets and the complete works of Paul Simon. Good luck so." He was very good about returning things. You always got the exact same number of records back. You'd never seen most of them before in your life.

Thanks to him I've got records in my collection which I wouldn't even buy in a plain brown paper bag. Max Bygraves and Barry Manilow. All the B-sides ever recorded by The Beverly Sisters. I'd die of shame if anybody ever saw them. God alone knows who has got mine.

I've been trying to get a pair of brown boots back since I left them under a hotel bed in Galway in 1976. A friend of mine was coming to Dublin the following weekend to see his girlfriend. My boots went up and down between the two cities for the next three years under the seat of his car. Then he left them under the bed in his girlfriend's flat. She went off to Spain to teach English and the boots went with her. I don't think I'll ever see them again.

*

For God's Sake Stop Being So Helpful

I had a brilliant case prepared. Bring the record back to the shop and explain that the needle keeps jumping on it. Tell them that I've got a brand new stereo so it couldn't possibly be the needle Then wait until the record plays perfectly in the shop. That was the bit that always left me without a leg to stand on.

This time I had my lines carefully rehearsed. "Fair enough. The record plays perfectly in here so in future every time I wish to listen to it, I'll bring it into the shop and my friends and I can sit around, drinking coffee and enjoying the music." The man in the shop ruined everything. He apologised for all the inconvenience, said that there must be something wrong with my record and offered to change it for me on the spot. I was speechless. All my lovely lines were gone to waste. People in shops aren't supposed to be as helpful as that. I don't know what's going on at all.

I complained to a switchboard operator for leaving me hanging on for ages. That's usually good for a rip roaring row. She was so understanding that I was utterly bewildered. She understood my position perfectly and apologised for the frustration which the delay must have caused me. I'm not programmed to handle stuff like that. I'm living in a world which is leaving me fewer and fewer things to give out about. A priest admitted to me yesterday that in many ways the church has failed to move with the times. I felt like explaining to him that he was using my lines. I'm supposed to be the one who says that and then we both blitz each other with bits out of scripture. I tried it on with a doctor recently. I told him the way that alternative medicine had worked wonders with my asthma. That one was always good for at least ten three-minute rounds. Not only did this guy agree with all the alternative ideas, he even offered to loan me a few books on the subject. The first politician to cop on to this new thinking will go straight to the top. None of them had ever had a good word to say about the opposition. They blame one another for everything. It's only a matter of time before one of them says it. "I agree completely with the leader of the opposition. Every word he says is true. My party feels thoroughly ashamed of itself. I don't know how the Irish public puts up with us." It's a winner. It leaves the opposition utterly legless. Go for it, lads and lassies.

*

Russian Roulette With The Record Player

I haven't bought myself a compact disc player yet. I don't think that I really want one. If I had my way I'd still be putting my Delia Murphy '78s onto the green baize turntable and watching them hurtle around at breakneck speed. Me and my brothers used to stand our lead soldiers around the edges of 'The Roving Journeymen' and Delia would send them whizzing all over the room. If I can find a compact disc player which plays old '78s with lovely crackly noises I might just be tempted. I've got a sound system which plays vinyl and cassette tapes. It is sleek and black and modern but as far as I'm concerned I'd rather have the record player that I bought with my first wage packet.

It was a glorious big boxy yoke and you loaded it up with eight records at a time. You piled on your Elvis, Buddy Holly and Rick Nelson singles and you clamped them into place with the metal arm.

The theory couldn't have been simpler. You sat back and relaxed and listened to eight consecutive singles without lifting a finger.

Some of the records were shaped like Frisbees and others caved in towards the middle. Some of them curled up at the edges while others looked perfectly OK. You never knew when it was going to happen. Suddenly two misshapen records coincided on the turntable. They snarled and skidded and scraped together and you shot across the room before the needle hacked lumps out of 'Peggy Sue Got Married.'

There were lots of metal parts on my first record player. Trying to operate it was like playing Russian roulette with a power station. Sometimes you touched the speed selector and electric tingles shot up as far as your armpits.

Sometimes you adjusted the volume and the hairs on the back of your hand crackled. My brother wouldn't go anywhere near it unless he was wearing my mother's rubber gloves and his own crepe-soled shoes. It was the beginning of the end for me when they got rid of the '78 speed. I was shattered. I tried putting my Delia Murphy records on at 45rpm and then spinning the turntable around faster with my hand. Little black slivers flew off the disc and embedded themselves in the far wall, so I had to stop before I blinded somebody.

God be with the days when His Master's dog stared into a horn and there were 78 revolutions in a minute. Next thing you know they'll be taking away our 33 speed and then where will we be?

*

When Carpets Make Leg Hair Crackle

My legs felt funny. One moment they were fine. Then I walked into a record shop and they felt all heavy and leaden. Suddenly

I was walking like Mr Plod, the village policeman. My first thoughts were dramatic ones. "If this it, if I am to be struck down in my prime in a Dublin record shop, fare thee well noble legs and thank you for everything." I didn't panic. I'm proud of that. I didn't shout, "Somebody alert the flying doctor, I'm losing the use of my legs!" I didn't crumple to the floor and deliver a speech about Yorick. I plodded out of the shop in dignified silence.   It felt just like wading through molten porridge in a pair of deep-sea diver's boots. As soon as my feet touched the pavement outside the shop, my legs were reborn. They felt perfect again. I felt the need to apologise to them. "Legs, I overreacted a bit in there. Sorry, it won't happen again. You have my word on that."

It had to be the carpet. Perhaps it's some kind of fiendish plan for keeping people in the shop until they buy something. Supermarkets do it with subliminal suggestion. Maybe record shops do it with sticky carpets.

I told a security man what had happened. He was standing in a shop doorway with his walkie-talkie and nobody was telling him anything. So I did. He explained to me about anti-static carpets. "They prevent people who walk into the shop from overloading the vinyl or affecting the computers." I honestly never realised that my feet posed such a threat to advanced technology.

I stood outside the next record shop for a long time. I was wondering whether or not they'd mind me standing at the threshold and testing their carpet one leg at a time. Two teenage girls were on their way out so I asked them, "Excuse me, before you both come out, would you ever mind stopping for a moment and sensing into your legs? I'm not being personal or anything like that, but do they feel kind of porridgy?"

I told them I was half-afraid to go in because my own legs had been partially porridged earlier on.   They were very obliging. The pair of them took their time and sensed into their legs and told me grand. There was no porridge.

A carpet in a computer showroom in London made the hairs on my legs crackle last year. But that was different. I thoroughly enjoyed every crackle.

*

Turning On The Supermarket

I nearly died of fright when I walked into the supermarket. The first thing I heard was very heavy breathing. The sort of thing you hear on your television at two in the morning when you don't have a scrambler but the sound is still coming through. Somebody somewhere in the supermarket was obviously having the time of their life. Then a very husky female voice said "Bien" as if she really meant it before lapsing into the rapturous breathing again. "My goodness," I thought. "If that girl's mammy comes in here now to buy a packet of Rice Crispies she'll send her straight up to bed without any dinner." It seemed to be coming from behind the tins of catfood. And the sliced pans. And the kitten soft toilet rolls. It was only then I realised they were playing the song *Je t'Aime* as background music. Jane Birkin was puffing and panting like a chronic attack of asthma. She was singing all sorts of throaty things in French and they certainly weren't special offers. I was starting to feel the kind of mounting excitement which is not normally given to men of my age.

I veered over towards the cold foods cabinet with my trolley and opened the door. A cloud of dry ice wafted up around me and restored my body to the state of grace. I grabbed a packet of chicken curry pancakes and fled. When I got home and put away my shopping I lay down for a while. My system was in deep shock. This is not the sort of thing you expect in the middle of the afternoon. One hour later I felt ready to face the world again. I went downstairs and telephoned my building society to check up on my repayments. The girl on the switchboard asked me to hold on for a couple of seconds. Then the recorded music came throbbing down the line. The hypnotic rhythm of Ravel's "Bolero" triggered off little electrical tingles in my ear-lobes. Jane Birkin experiencing broncho-spasm in the supermarket was bad enough. But Bo Derek flashbacks from the building society were more than my body could stand. I was manfully fighting off wild action replays from the film '10' when the telephonist came back on the line.

"For pity's sake," I pleaded. "Don't ever play Ravel to me again. 'Greensleeves' or 'An English Country Garden' or any hymn of your choice but not that!" Then I went upstairs and lay down again. It comes to us all with age.

*

Why Trying Not To Look Is A Lot Harder Than Just Looking

Sometimes I find it very hard not to look. I was standing outside a department store last week, waiting for a friend. A young woman appeared in the shop window behind me and started to whip the clothes off every one of the models. In a matter of moments there wasn't a stitch on any of them. Then she disappeared again. Maybe she was gone for her tea-break or something. She left me standing there in front of a window filled with haughty-looking models who would have frozen to death if they had been human. I didn't want to be looking and that's the mistake I made. The harder you try not to do something, the greater the tension. Lot's wife was turned into a pillar of salt for less.

It's the same thing when you're speeding home on the DART after dark. All the houses have their lights on, and lots of them don't even bother to draw their curtains. It would make life an awful lot easier all round if they did. If anybody stared into my upstairs windows from a passing train, I'd be full of self-righteous indignation, yet here I am whizzing along on the

DART chancing the occasional sideways glance. If you were suddenly solidified into a lump of table salt, you'd have to stay there until a couple of strong people lifted you out at the terminus.

Couples shouldn't be allowed to massage one another in shop doorways beside a bus queue. Everyone in the queue is concentrating on staring straight ahead and keeping their eyes locked into the forward position. Meanwhile in the doorway, arms are under coats, and coats are under arms, and the hardest time of all not to see anything is when you're concentrating like mad on not looking. I can remember when all the cart horses in Dublin used to wear blinkers. I don't think they ever knew how well off they were.

*

I Believed You, Did You Believe Me?

We knew very little about them. They all went to the girls' school. They all stood together on the far side of the dance floor. They cried when you upset them. They fancied Gerry O'Keefe and you couldn't stand him. Yet you knew the day was going to come when you would have to go out with one of them.

There was nobody to ask. We pretended that we knew everything there was to know. We stood around the school yard nudging and winking at one another and none of us had the faintest idea what we were nudging and winking about. "Did I ever what? ! Sure you know yourself!" And we all nodded and wondered what the hell it was we were supposed to know ourselves.

Suddenly you were standing outside Clery's for the very first time. It was nearly 7.30pm. Oh God — she'll be here any minute. Part of you was hoping that she wouldn't turn up. Your mind was working overtime trying to think of something brilliant to say. Any second now. Check your reflection in the window. Suddenly she is there standing in front of you. You are concentrating so hard on looking and sounding relaxed that you don't notice she is doing exactly the same. You start to talk and she starts to talk and you both stop and there is very loud silence and you have forgotten all the brilliant things you were going to say. "You're here," She agrees with you that she is here. You both establish the fact that you are here and neither of you knows where to go from there.

She looks beautiful and you feel terrified. This is not the same as standing in the school yard making knowing noises with the other lads. She is here and she is a real young woman and you can nod and wink all you like but it is not going to help you now. Do I take her hand or does she tuck her arm into mine or what? Oh Mammy ...

Sitting in the half-light of the cinema. I wonder should we be holding hands yet. That guy over there. He has got his arm around his girl. Still, maybe they've married. That's different. How do I get my arm around without her noticing what I'm doing? Maybe she thinks I'm too slow. Then again if I make a move now I might be too fast. Do I just grab hold of her hand or do I say something romantic first or what? I wonder what lipstick tastes like. I wonder if I'll ever know.

I'd love to meet the lads again. I'd love to ask them. Did you really believe that I knew as much as I pretended to? Because I believed you.

*

I Didn't Mean It

I have never deliberately tried to make a car crash. Nothing is further from my mind. Yet at least two car crashes have happened simply because I was standing on the pavement. About ten years ago I was waiting for a bus at the bottom of Vernon Avenue. I wasn't thinking about cars. I wasn't even looking at them. Suddenly I heard a screech of brakes and a thud. A car had braked very quickly and a man on a Honda 50 ran into the back of it. The driver of the car was in bits. He explained to me that he had only stopped to tell me that he couldn't give me a lift because he was turning right at the next corner.

Last summer I was standing at a bus stop on Grace Park Road. It was a lovely sunny morning and once again cars were the furthest thing from my mind. A sudden gust of wind tried to blow my hat off and I raised my hand smartly to grab it. A passing taxi driver thought that I was flagging him down and jammed on the brakes. There was an unmerciful crashing sound as the car behind him whammed into the back of his taxi. I nearly had a heart attack with the fright of it. I honestly didn't mean it.

About four year ago I got into a taxi at the Lansdowne Road rank and told the driver where I wished to go. Then I made a perfectly harmless remark about something and the driver took exception to what I had said. Suddenly the atmosphere wasn't one in which I would wish to travel so I asked him to stop and let me out. He stopped and went into a very angry. There was an unmerciful bump as he ran into the front of the first taxi on the rank. Once again I swear to God that I didn't do it on purpose.

I was waiting for a bus in the lashing rain last year on the Clontarf Road. A car stopped and the couple in it very kindly offered me a lift into town. I was thrilled. We laughed and joked all the way to Dame Street. Everything was lovely. Then I got out of their car and banged the door shut behind me. To my astonishment the window fell out and broke on the roadway. I apologised profusely. I really did. I don't think that cars like me very much.

I have only crashed a car from the inside once. During my first driving lesson in Luton the Morris 1100 which I was driving suddenly shot forward and rammed a Mini. My instructor was amazed. "How the hell did you do that?" he asked. I wasn't able to tell him because I honestly didn't know. It just happened. I travel everywhere by bus now. I think it's much fairer to all concerned.

*

Looking For The Life Of Reilly

Sometimes I think I'd like a nice easy job. One with no problems or pressure. I wouldn't mind being a van driver's helper for a while. Sitting up front in the cab and looking out the window. Standing behind the van when it's reversing into tight corners shouting: "Left hand down a bit Marty."

I wouldn't mind being a ladder holder either. All you have to do is hold onto both sides of it and place your right foot on the third rung. You don't have to say technical things, but you do have to keep looking upwards and, once every 20 minutes, say something like — "Okay ...no sweat ... I got it."

I think that the job of ladder holder is under threat at the moment. Last week, in Fairview, I saw a ladder with a heavy cement bag wedged against the bottom. This is not good enough. If this sort of thing catches on we will have cement bags sitting beside van drivers in cabs and then where will we be?

Whenever things get too much for me I always think longingly about an easy job where I don't have to worry. But in the past, whenever I took refuge in a simple situation, it drove me crazy after a couple of days. Nothing could be easier than placing a Mars Bar into every Selection Box which moves past on a conveyor belt. There I was saying to myself — "No more problems ... I'm made for life."

After two or three days, I was speaking to myself under my breath in nursery rhymes and asking traffic lights to marry me. I think you can only do the same thing for so long and then golf umbrellas start to look out at you from the bathroom mirror and tell you secrets.

I remember a counsellor once saying to me that it's never too late to completely change your life around. There is nothing you cannot do if you put your mind to it. That being so, I have decided to either drive a train or play in goals for Ireland.

I can bring a bit of wisdom into the back four and fuse them into a purposeful unit with quotations from *The Prophet*.

Whenever my hamstring plays me up and I need to sit down for a while, I can drive goods trains full of cows to Nenagh or anywhere else they wish to go. *Iarnrod Eireann* can point to my lack of experience if they like but that sort of negative thinking never got us anywhere. They've got miles and miles of railway tracks which they never use. I can practice on them until I get the hang of the brakes. And then it's full steam ahead.

*

Think Of A Number Between...

I once worked for Vauxhall Motors in Luton. One day an instruction came from General Motors in America. "We want to know how much of everything you've got over there so get your act together and count it."

Anybody who looked remotely like they could count past one hundred found themselves reporting to the Inventory Department. We were given a crash course on how to supervise the counting of rivets and ratchets and washers and little teenchy things which hold cars together. We were shown how to enter the exact number and type of the teenchy things on the official inventory forms and how to initial our answers. Then we were given white coats and released on the factory.

I had never been a supervisor before. I had never been placed in charge of anybody in my whole life. The two men who had been assigned to me as official counters thought it would be a good idea to start by counting the factory. "Right lad," they said. "We've got one of that." Then they suggested counting me.

This was certainly not the spirit which had made General Motors great. So I pointed towards a gigantic bin which contained millions and millions of little roundy metal yokes. "OK men. We'll start with those. Perhaps you'd be good enough to count them for me and then I'll enter your answer on the form and initial it."

The two men took turns in telling me all sorts of things which I could do. They suggested manoeuvres which involved flag-poles, spiral staircases and jockeys' saddles. They proposed creative combinations which included coconuts trampolines and Nelson's Column. Then out of the blue, one of them said — "Six million, three hundred thousand, four hundred and sixty three. No, I tell a lie — sixty-four." The last thing I wished to be was ungracious. All things considered it seemed to be a fairly constructive guess.

General Motors would probably be thrilled to hear that they had that many little roundy metal yokes over in Luton. From that moment on we carried out our section of the inventory with the express purpose of thrilling the top management over in Detroit. We filled in millions of square bits, trillions of triangular things with holes in them, zillions of tiny wobbly springs. And I signed for them all. Wobbly springs is right.

*

Have You Ever Seen Indigumble?

I was staring into the middle distance in the cafe. I was trying to work something out in my mind. "Cheer up . . . it might never happen," a man said to me. I told him it wasn't like that at all. "I'm simply trying to work out what colour my rasher is."

There was nothing wrong with the rasher either. That is why I had refrained from calling a waitress over and saying — "What colour would you say this rasher is?" She would have thought I was being smart or complaining or something, and I wasn't. She might have even dashed off and got me another one. That would only have made matters worse because I couldn't work out the colour of the one that I'd got.

I had already asked the security man what colour would he say my baked beans were. He looked at them for a while and he said orange. I wasn't really happy with his answer because they certainly didn't look orange to me. They seemed to be a colour for which there is no official name. So I stared into the middle distance until I thought of one.

Winamburple. A mixture of wine and amber and purple. That is what colour I thought the beans were. But if you told someone a thing like that they would only lock you up. It was exactly the same with my rasher. Mauvurple. A mixture of mauve and purple. But you can't go through life telling people that you have got a mauvurple rasher. They will only go and sit at another table.

I am OK on black and white. I honestly thought I was fine on all the other colours as well. But I wandered into the employment office of Irish Rail many years ago to apply for a job as a railway porter. I had just spent four years in England where you wandered into a different personnel office every week and filled up a few forms and you were working in a brand new job the following Monday.

I had no trouble filling in my name and address and stuff like that. Then they gave me a chart with lots of colours on it.

I started to write down their names as I saw them. Ambink. Indigumble. Purange. That is exactly how they seemed to me. God alone knows how I would see the signals if I was driving a train. The railway people seemed to think that I would even wreak havoc wandering up and down a platform with a sweeping brush.

So I write. The words are black. The paper is white. There are no bleens or breds or gruples. I do get the occasional indigumble but then I suppose you can't have everything.

*

Trying To Find The Right Forest

Sometimes I think that I would like to have a proper job. I haven't had one since 1964. It was the kind of job where you got paid every week. You were sure of your money. An old man came round every Friday with a tray of brown envelopes and he gave you one and it was filled with notes and coins. Everybody sat at their desk and counted their money and paid one another back any cash which they'd borrowed. Then you started work again and waited for the old man to come round again next Friday. If you got sick for a while, they still paid you. You could lie in bed with the flu and feel cosy because Mr Grogan was still going to fill your envelope with notes and coins while you were getting better. You could go away and relax on a beach in Spain for three weeks because you knew that he was in Dublin putting rubber bands around your envelopes and keeping them safe for you until you got back. Every year that you stayed in the job, your envelope got fatter. It seemed like a great arrangement. The only problem was that you had to go in there every day. You couldn't ring them up and say, "It's such a lovely morning that I think I'll go into the woods in Malahide and collect lots of acorns. I'll see you tomorrow or the next day." You couldn't ring in and say, "I met this incredible Dutch girl in a pub last night and she has asked me to head off to Connemara with her for three weeks to live in her tent. Will you ask Mr Grogan to mind my envelopes for me or better still, could he send them on to the post office in Clifden?"

Insurance companies didn't have arrangements like that for their junior clerks. I kept meeting these travel-stained French and German teenagers who had just hit Dublin after living on a beach in Santorini. They didn't seem to be worried about brown envelopes or Mr Grogan or anything. After their next pint of Guinness, they were heading off to meditate half-way up a mountain in India.

Every time I thought about leaving the job, a voice in my head warned me about skid row, the poorhouse, being washed up, down and out and written off. It hasn't happened yet but you never completely lose that nagging worry. You can collect all the acorns you like, but if Mr Grogan is still lurking behind the occasional tree, you haven't fully found the right forest.

*

Warm Baths And Liquorice Allsorts

We never stop asking one another. "Still hard at it?" The response is supposed to be — "Up to my eyes . I haven't got a second." Then the person tells you — "That's a good complaint." We have reached the point where we actually believe all that stuff. Our sense of personal worth becomes dependent on how hectically busy we are. "Life is powerful right now — I'm run off my feet. I hardly had time to think today."

I decided to do nothing, about two weeks ago. I didn't even put a time-limit on it. From this moment on I'm going to do nothing and see what it's like. So far it has been brilliant, "There ye are-still hard at it" "No I'm not doing anything at all." "That's terrible-I really am sorry to hear it."

'It's not it's fabulous." "Oh-I see-you were utterly run off your feet so you decided to have a hard-earned holiday." "No-I wasn't doing a tap so I decided to sort of concentrate on it from now on "

All of a sudden people don't know what to say anymore. All of a sudden they can't tell me what a good complaint it is. Straight away they kick to touch. "Ah yes but I'd say you've got loads of really hard graft coming up. That's not quite as good as being run off your feet but it is still fairly reasonable grounds for complaint "No ... there's not a thing in the pipeline." "God — that's dreadful — how are you coping?" "Well, yesterday afternoon I lay in a lovely warm bath and ate a pound of liquorice allsorts." At that stage people usually scurry away as fast as they can for fear of catching whichever social disease has struck you down.

You're not supposed to enjoy the weekend unless you have slaved away for the rest of the week. You're not supposed to enjoy your dessert unless you have waded through your main course first. You are not supposed to enjoy your life unless you have earned the right by running yourself off your feet. Right now I'm not hard at anything. I'm hearing birdsongs again. I'm noticing the shapes of clouds. I have emptied the pipeline and it's full of liquorice allsorts. It's a delicious complaint.

*

How To Utterly Screw Up Your Next Interview

I think that job interviewers hold all the aces. They know that you are not really likely to interrupt them or disagree or argue or anything like that. If you are not careful you will become such a polite and correct person during the interview that your own mother wouldn't let you pass the front door because she wouldn't know you from Adam.

From time to time it is a liberating feeling to really extend your interviewer. Upon entering his office suddenly swing around on your heel and command an imaginary dog to "Sit!" Give the command very sharply. Then brandish your finger and warn — "If you attack that nice man over there even once my lad it's no juicy bones for you with your supper!" Then sit down.

Don't say a word. Wait and see how your interviewer responds to the presence of a dog in his office which he cannot see. This will tell you a great deal about the calibre of the person with whom you are dealing. He may or may not refer to the dog depending on how easy he is with himself as an interviewer. If the interview proceeds as normal, and it very well might, it is a fascinating exercise to conduct yourself with deep seriousness for a while. Talk about intervention beef annual shortfalls and personal development. Talk about regional funds, bottom lines and ultimate sanctions. Very suddenly, even when you are least expecting it, spring up as high as you can out of your chair and when you are at your highest point shout very triumphantly — "Hike!" When you land again carry on talking about expanding into European markets exactly as you were before take-off. At this point the job is probably well and truly gone. People who rise up vertically out of chairs exclaiming "Hike" or "Hup" usually talk themselves out of all the best positions. But you are doing your interviewer a deep and abiding favour. We all need to be thrown unexpectedly upon our inner resources and have our capability put to the sternest test. He may even thank you for it.

If you perform several "Hikes" at irregular intervals, the interviewer may well find himself unconsciously trying to anticipate your next one. This is a great way of building up dramatic tension.   Rising slowly to your feet singing "The Flowers That Bloom In The Spring Tra La" while dancing with Lady Arabella Fingleton, especially if she is not there is a powerful way of getting his full attention and taking his mind off your next "Hike."

On the other hand you may elect to behave throughout with dignity. Whichever course you choose I wish you total success.
*

Kindly Stuff Your Rubbish Somewhere Else

I don't mind the postman doing it. As far as I'm concerned he can push things through my letterbox anytime his job warrants it. I have met him and I like him. He comes nice and early in the morning and I think that my letterbox likes him too.   I have never actually caught the other people in the act.

I have no idea where they come from or when exactly they do it. I wish to God that they'd stop. I don't want little boxes of Rice-Crispies rammed in through my letterbox. My message is simple and clear. Kindly shove your miniature parcels of breakfast cereal anywhere else that you feel creatively inclined. I don't want them.   I also don't want my roof tiled or my gutters repaired or anything like that. My gutters are lovely. So is my roof. I love them just the way they are. Sometimes I even go outside and sing this message up to them. Once again I don't know who these people are. Perhaps they hide outside in the bushes until they see me going out.   Every so often somebody feels the need to let me know that they've got a warehouse full of women's clothing at knock-down prices. Even if you are giving the stuff away for nothing I don't want women's clothing thank you very much. I have checked with each of my three cats in turn. They don't want any either.

People who manufacture margarine are always at it. They can't stay away from my letterbox. Sometimes I'm knee deep in '15p Off Your Next Purchase' leaflets. I'd much rather have the cash. Honestly. If you haven't got the right money just post in a five pound note and we can sort out the change next time you call round.

Nobody ever came near me during my days in flatland. Many's the time I would have eaten a little bowlful of rice-crispies, cardboard and all. Gutters leaked and tiles fell off roofs but nobody wanted to know. I don't creep around to TDs' houses in the dead of night and stuff their letterboxes full of poems. And yet sometimes I open my front door and the little boxes of rice-crispies are buried under piles of leaflets which are all telling me different ways to vote. The TDs even put their photographs on the leaflets. They all seem to get their hair styled and blow-dried first. I'm sure that their wives think they look lovely. I don't. They remind me of my days in insurance. Unless you are the postman kindly stay away from my letterbox or I'll set the cats on you.

*

A Fantasy Of Fluffies

I used to dread it. Sitting alone at my typewriter for hours at a stretch. No sense of occasion. I wanted to be like visiting soccer teams when they come to Dublin. They run onto the pitch before the match begins and put their hands up over their heads. Then they applaud their supporters.

I rounded up all of my fluffies. I've got millions of rabbits and dogs and penguins which I've won in amusement arcades. Then

I stood some empty bookshelves beside my desk and packed them with a capacity crowd of stuffed toys. Suddenly I had a grandstand filled with fans.

There was still something missing. There's not much point in trotting towards the typewriter and applauding the fluffies if they just sit there and look at you. You need some kind of mass hysteria. I borrowed a sound-effects disc from RTE and put it onto tape. It's a brilliant tape of 35,000 soccer fans enjoying an English FA cup match. There's nothing like it. Now I simply hit the button on my tape deck and the atmosphere is electric. I do a lap of honour around my desk and the fluffies roar their heads off .

It still didn't feel completely authentic. There was no warm-up. If you wander into a soccer stadium half an hour before kick-off, you'll see both teams out on the pitch doing their exercises. They run forwards and backwards and sideways. Sometimes they lie on their backs and pedal imaginary bikes. That's what was missing.

I had a brief tactical talk with my fingers. "None of you is going anywhere near that typewriter from now on until you have done your exercises." Then I took them for a training run around my Subuteo pitch with loud shouts of "Hup, Hup" to encourage them. I ran them sideways and back-to-front. I jumped them up and down. Then I stood them to attention and sang the National Anthem. Only then did I treat them to the sound of 35,000 wildly cheering fluffies.

Lots of writers don't take their fingers seriously enough. Sportspeople are always rubbing stuff into their legs. Sometimes they sit on the ground and stare at their knees. Sometimes the trainer pummels their thighs for them and there's no harm in it. We can make a start by rubbing Vick or something into our fingers.
*

I Quadruple Dare You

We used to look at the big bell every day. It was set into the wall outside the Fire Station in Buckingham Street. We began by daring one another. "Go on — I double-dare you. Ring it and all the firemen will come whizzing down the golden pole and the fire engine will come bursting out through the doors and they'll go clanging away down the road looking for big puffs of smoke." Treble-dares didn't work either. It was the million trillion-times dare which finally coaxed Gerry Murtagh to creep up and put his finger on it. A head appeared suddenly out of a window across the road and roared at us to 'Get to hell outta that' and we didn't stop running until we were safely inside the school yard.

We also flirted with the red communication cord on the train. We reached up and tipped it. We wrapped our fingers very gently around it and applied a tiny bit of pressure. We touched it and tipped it. We discussed it and debated it. We even invented a million-trillion-zillion-times dare which evaporated into thin-air when Michael Brady told us what his father had said. Mr Brady worked on Howth Junction Station so he knew all about trains. He said that if any of us even looked sideways at that cord, every single brake on the train would wham up against the wheels and the train would skid for miles with showers of red sparks all around it. Then, he said, we would all be taken away to prison in vans with bars on the windows and we'd have to wear prickly convict suits covered with little upside-down arrows, our families would be disgraced and we'd all be eating stale bread and drinking cold soup with black things floating in it.

So we just sat there in the carriage secretly hoping for an emergency like a very old lady getting locked into the toilet or cowboys with bandanas over their faces pounding along the roof. I even had a recurring nightmare where I fell out of the luggage rack and accidentally grabbed the cord and the whole carriage was suddenly filled with judges who wore cross faces and powdery wigs.

We are now surrounded by a plethora of things which we must not push or pull or press. Whenever I ride on an escalator I am extra-specially careful about where I rest my hands. I avoid open-plan offices whose ceilings are peppered with sprinklers in case my body-heat triggers off a deluge. I never even look sideways at little red hammers in glass boxes. I plan my route carefully so that I never find myself walking past fire stations. It takes me ages to get home but it's worth it.

*

How In The Name Of God Did They Get There?

There is an extra-special time which only happens once or twice each month. It is a time in the middle of the night when the whole country is either sound asleep, down caves or tunnels, under the stairs, stuck in lifts or under deep hypnosis. That is the time when they erect the big towering building-site cranes. I have questioned countless people. None of them has ever actually seen it being done. Neither have they witnessed the same cranes being taken down. One man even crouched inside a bird-watching hide near a building site for two whole weeks. He nipped out to do a wee wee and by the time he got back, the huge crane was miraculously in position. A little hand-written note was pinned to his hide. "Tee hee ... bah jeerie bah ... serves you right."

The men who erect the cranes are sworn to secrecy. Nobody knows who they are. They have got special handshakes, code words, and go to bed at night with masking tape over their mouths so they won't talk in their sleep.

Their wives believe that they work as pork butchers, art critics or trouser-pressers. None of these men know the whole proce-dure. So if they are ever captured and tickled under their feet with feathers they would be unable to explain in full how it is done. I believe that the erection of one of these mighty cranes involves a working knowledge of Honours, Latin, Russian Helicopters, Levitation, Bolivian Folk-dance, Minced Pies and Dynamic Tension. I further believe that the gigantic concrete blocks at the end of each crane are raised by Nubian slaves who work on contract. They use ancient tackle, strong mules, hand-woven ropes and biblical chants.

I believe that in order to work as a crane driver it is necessary to take a degree course in the art of Zen and Advanced Bladder Control. Once they are perched up high in their dizzy cabs they mediate on a Burmese Mantra which in translation says — "I do not need to do a wee wee therefore I am."

I cannot understand how enterprising promoters like Jim Aitken and Pat Egan have not stumbled on to the ultimate money-spinning event. The world and his wife would happily pay top prices to watch one of those cranes being put together. They would need the vastest venue this country has ever seen. It would have to be — 'Live At The Curragh' because nowhere else is big enough. As long as they don't frighten the race horses or the sheep I don't see how anybody could possibly object.

*

Behind You!

The child is still in every one of us. The very same child who happily roared his head off at the pantomime. It's only dying to get the same chance again. "Oh yes it is!" "Oh no it's not!" "Look out behind ye!" The tape is still programmed into your subconscious and it's raring to go.

I find it very hard to remain silent during 'The Playboy of The Western World'. I have to fight back the urge to shout at the top of my voice — "That widow woman is only after you for your body Christy!" Somebody should tell him. Godot is worse. It's about time somebody in the audience put poor Estragon and

Vladimir out of their misery. "He's not coming lads and that is bloody well that. You can fiddle with your boots for as long as you like but you're only wasting your time and ours as well so would you ever give us a bar of a song or something!"

I have no problem about remaining silent during 'Julius Caesar'. Perhaps other people feel like tipping him off. "Would you for God's sake listen to your wife Julius — that woman knows what she is talking about!" I spent three hard years with the Christian Brothers slogging through his Gallic Wars so as far as I'm concerned, the guy deserves all that he gets.

Lots of us are only waiting to be asked. I think it's about time for Hamlet to edge towards the front of the stage and plead with his audience — "Will somebody for God's sake tell me — what IS the question?' and we all shout back — "To be or not to be!" Then he pretends to be deaf and says "I can't hear you," and we all have to roar it even louder. I find it very hard to warm to Portia. Just when you think you're going to see a decent bit of blood on the stage she takes Shylock apart in court and he has to put away his knife. The whole thing is just warming up nicely. There you are wondering how are they going to reduce Antonio's weight by exactly one pound without finishing him off altogether. And then she wrecks everything. I was brought up on a staple diet of Hammer Horror movies. The kind of films where Shylock would be waggling his knife and asking the audience — "Will I or won't I?" And the women in the seat beside you who looks like a triple daily communicant suddenly shows herself in her true colours by yelling — "Go for it Shylock! Go for it!"

*

Hi Ho My Head

My body was quivering with anticipation. I never thought that I'd find a video like it. I felt like running all the way home. The last time that I saw The Lone Ranger was when we had our very first black-and-white television set. He used to talk to scoundrels in black hats about justice and fair play. He fired silver bullets which never actually hit anybody. He addressed women in flowery bonnets as "Ma'am" and never said things like "Your place or mine"   He was forever sending his trusty sidekick Tonto into town to find out whatever he could about crooked ranchers, sneaky rustlers, bent sheriffs and anybody else who wore a black hat and a stubble to match. Tonto was always being whacked over the head with iron bars for his troubles but he never once complained. He was a peace-loving brave who never did war-dances, wore coloured eye-shadow or galloped round and round wagon trains yelling "Scalp the lot of them."

I almost wept with relief. The Lone Ranger still cares. Ten minutes into my video and already he knew that the wealthy cattle baron was up to no good. Everyone else was fooled, including the governor of the state. I was even yelling at the screen "Don't trust him ... he's trying to get all the Indians wiped out because he wants to get his greedy hands on the silver in their Holy Mountain." But I needn't have worried. The Lone Ranger knew exactly what he was doing. He sent poor old obedient Tonto into town to listen outside windows and doorways. Minutes later the unfortunate Indian was being strung up in the main street by a lynch mob with an attitude problem and black stubbles. You knew exactly what Tonto was thinking: "Fair enough — this may be plenty bad but any second now there will be silver bullets flying round all over the place and Kemo Sabay will do the needful without actually hurting anybody." Before rescuing Tonto, the man in the black mask made time to single-handedly put down a Red Indian uprising by challenging Angry Lion to a fair fight without weapons or kicking or pulling each other's hair. Even when Angry Lion grabbed a spear, The Lone Ranger told him that we can't possibly create a just society if you insist on lunging at me with that sort of thing.

I slept easier in my bed last night. Help is only a silver bullet away.
*

Please Die Without The Music

Sad films make me cry. The first time that I saw Shenandoah I had to be assisted from the cinema. When James Stewart wandered out to his wife's grave and started talking to her I was in bits. Every time he called her 'Martha', my sobbing made my ribs vibrate. People around me in the cinema kept telling me: " It's only a film." But it wasn't only a film to me. It was a lonely man grieving for the completeness which once was his. Her name was Martha.

I was watching Fiddler on the Roof at home. I was fine when Topol was singing to his cows. But as soon as he started to get misty-eyed and sing with pride about his daughters I was gone. My tears were splashing onto the beanbag. Then my doorbell rang. There was a young guy outside who told me he was selling lines for £1 each to help people with head injuries. Under normal circumstances that wouldn't have touched me too deeply. But Topol had just activated my tear ducts and the reservoir was open. I started to think about people with their heads swathed in bandages and all of a sudden I was heartbroken. I bought ten lines. The young guy couldn't believe it.

I began crying during the sad bits at a very early age. Ben Bono and his travelling fit-up show came to Malahide every summer. We used to sit in the tent every night watching melodramas where landlords evicted pregnant women into blizzards. A violin would be playing in the wings. Paroxysms of grief would sweep through the audience. When poor Quasimodo was tied to a stake and all he wanted was a drop of water to wet his parched lips I wasn't able to go asleep until five o'clock the following morning.

People dying in films finish me off completely especially when they do it with music. I was watching a man dying in black and white with music in an old war film last week. His close friend was reminding him of his promise to buy the pair of them a couple of steaks when the war was over. The wounded man raised himself onto one elbow and with his last breath whispered — "with two fried eggs". Then the music swelled up and he died. I haven't been the better of it since. Why can't they just die and say nothing? It would be a lot easier on all of us.

*

Back In The Days When TV Shrank And Spun

Our black and white television set used to do terrible things to us. It had a whole range of built-in special effects over which we had very little control. Sometimes the whole family would be watching 'Laramie.' Just when it was getting to the most exciting bit, the entire picture began to scrunch itself up. It was almost as if an invisible pair of hands was squeezing everything in from both sides. Suddenly the 14 inch picture was reduced down to seven, and getting smaller by the second. "Quick Da quick ... Slim is going to be shot ... we'll miss it." With one bound my father was over beside the TV and twirling a little knob at the back. "No Da, No ... the other way. The whole picture is squinched up in the middle now." Inch by inch my father twirled it the other way and slowly stretched 'Laramie' back out toward the edges of the screen. Then he stood there watching it for a few seconds. As soon as he felt that he could trust it again he sat back into his seat.
The tension was unbelievable. We never took a programme for granted because at any second it was likely to be scrunched. Sometimes it squeezed in from the top and the bottom so that the picture was still 14 inches wide but it was only two inches tall. It wasn't only our television. All over Ireland people were leaping up and down from their seats and grappling with little buttons behind their sets. Our family called it the unscrunching

button, but the technical name was Vertical and Horizontal Hold. Sometimes our TV went into the slot machine mode where the picture began a wild spin. It whirled around at high speed and made the whole family dizzy. "No Da, no ... the other way ... it's going faster now." With masterly control my father slowed it down, and just as he was getting the brake onto 'Dixon of Dock Green' the whole programme went into a reverse spin and whirled around the other way. "Hang on Da — you've got a sideways shrink with a slow spin ... try a bit of reverse thrust with a little touch of hold."

Sometimes the screen was blitzed by spontaneous snow. Sometimes the woman down the road switched on her vacuum cleaner and covered our picture with crackly lines. Sometimes granny went out into the kitchen and listened to the radio instead. Sometimes we joined her.

*

Straight-forward, No Messing Transactions

Supermarkets do it. They have a special fast lane marked 'Baskets Only.' I want every mainline railway station in Ireland to follow suit. Let them provide a special ticket office window marked — 'Nice Simple Easy Straight-forward Transactions With No Messing.'

The other window can be designated — 'Reserved For The Kind Of Cretins Who Wish To Complicate Everything And Hold Up The Queue.'

I don't know where these people come from. They are usually travelling with an entire rugby team in tow. It should only take them a couple of seconds to exchange their travel warrants for tickets. But since the warrants were issued, six of the team have now insisted that they must travel with their backs to the locomotive, the entire front row wants to sit beside the window or they're going to sulk all the way to Cork, and the rest of the lads are demanding student discounts.

Give these people a ticket window all to themselves. Let them complicate things as much as they like. Appoint the most dithery clerk in the whole *Iarnrod Eireann* organisation to deal with them and slow them down so much that they miss their train. It serves them bloody well right.

Let every bank in Ireland do exactly the same. There are people wandering around this country who are not happy unless they are withdrawing wages for everyone on the building site. The carpenters want their money in pesetas because you can buy your lump hammer cheaper in Madrid, one of the brickies wants his wages in pennies because he wants to lay them along the Naas Road to raise funds for the Bricklayers Benevolent Fund, and everyone else wants nice new shiny coins with kingfishers on them.

These people must be stopped now. They are driving the rest of us crazy. They don't know how to go into a post office and buy one stamp. They spend their lives posting gooseberry tarts, surface mail, to Omsk. They don't know how to buy a simple ticket to Galway. They prefer to bring an under-15 hurling team with them.

They love asking questions. "Supposing I wanted to post a live hedgehog to myself by registered mail, would I need to buy a special envelope with little ventilation holes in it?"

Why not centralise the whole thing? Build a huge depot for them in the middle of the Curragh and let them drive one another crazy out there. The rest of us are due a break

*

Perplexed By Plastic

I hate talking to people through perspex windows. Sometimes I know that bank cashiers are trying to tell me something because I can see their lips moving. But I can't hear a word that they are saying. So I start to shout to make sure that they can hear me. Unfortunately, everybody else in the bank can hear me too. I think that each cash window should be fitted with stereophonic earphones and a perspex bubble which you place over your head. That way, it's between you and the cashier and nobody else.

I get very nervous when I have to put my lodgement into a sort of security compartment on my side of the counter. Then I whip my hand out as fast as I can before the cashier slides the hatch shut. I'm always terrified of meeting a psychopathic banker who is having a really bad day. One sudden wham of that hatch and you would never play table tennis again.   I was buying a ticket recently at a mainline railway station. I could only see the bottom half of the ticket clerk's face because there was a metal bar across the perspex window at eye level. Straight away I started to wonder if she could see all of me.   "Can you see all of my face?" I asked her through the round bit which you speak into. Her lips moved and I couldn't hear her but I recognised the word "pardon". After your first couple of perspex windows, you can pick out "Pardon?" and "What?" a mile off. A diesel locomotive started to rev up in the background so I really had to shout. "I CAN ONLY SEE YOUR FACE FROM THE NOSE DOWN. HOW MUCH OF MINE CAN YOU SEE?" "IF YOU BEND DOWN A BIT, I CAN SEE ALL OF IT!" she yelled. So I bent down and bought my ticket from a crouched position. Exchanges like that can follow you all the way to Sligo.   Sometimes you are in the bank and men wearing blue helmets sweep in with bags of money. Suddenly the doors are closed without as much as a by your-leave. Nobody asks you: "Excuse me, sir — do you mind very much if we lock you in here for a while?" They just do it. I had five minutes written out of my life like that last week. I could have been enjoying a meringue in a cake shop. I could have been listening to the birdsong in Fairview Park. I was locked into a bank instead.   It's happened to me a couple of times before. That's about 15 minutes of my life that the bank owes me. My time is money to me. Lots and lots of it. I'm posting off my first invoice to the bank in the morning. There could be a fortune in this.

*
Switchboard Secrets

They never give you their names. You never know who you are talking to. There must be thousands of people working in government departments. I'm quite sure they use each other's names when they're having a chat together. It's completely different when you phone in. The voice on the switchboard says "I'm putting you through to 'Index'. "Before you've got the chance to say, "Hold on a minute — there's nobody in the bloody world called 'Index', " your call is switched through. A voice says "Hello-Index". At this stage they ask you for your name which is fair enough. I always say "My name is Pat Ingoldsby — who am I talking to?" There's usually a pause. "Eh — this is 'Index'." It's nice and safe in a huge big government office telling people that you're called 'Index' or 'Cross-Reference'. You can't be pinned down for anything. You can make a complete donkey's hernia of the matter in hand and nobody has got a clue who you are. "Hello — I was on to your department a few minutes ago and the person who was sorting out my problem asked me to hold on for a second and she went away and I got so browned off holding on that I hung up and now I'm phoning in again." "Who were you speaking to?" "Somebody who kept telling me she is called 'Index'. Who am I speaking to now?" "You're through to 'Index' again." "The hell I am. You're not bloody 'Index'. I'd know her voice anywhere." What are they afraid of? Is there an official directive in government departments that states "Find out as much as you can about the caller but for God's sake don't say who you are"?
It's the same when you ring a hospital and they put you through to the ward. "Hello — this is Nurse Squiddledegillick speaking." They say their name in such a rush that you haven't got a clue who they are. Perhaps that's the way that they want it. Switchboards are worse. They hide behind the cloak of anonym-

ity and then do the most dreadful telephonic things to you. Switchboard operators should be obliged by law to give their names slowly and distinctly when they answer your call. That way you know exactly who has shafted you with an out-of-control tape which won't stop playing 'Greensleeves'. You've got the right so go for it. Start asking for names It's great crack once you get going.

*

Get Your Needles Out

We studied all the wrong things in primary school. The girls did knitting and needlework because they were learning their place. The boys did gardening with big heavy spades and forks. That was how it was going to be. We would never need to know anything about sewing or cooking or darning socks. That was for the girls, while we took care of the tough manly jobs.

The theory was simple. You lived at home until you got married. That way your mammy looked after everything. Then a beautiful continuum took place where your mother passed on the darning needle to your wife. It was a ceremony something like the Olympic flame or passing on the baton in a relay race. Then your marriage lasted forever. This left you free to ask questions like — "Where's my dinner?" and "Where did you put my clean socks"

My marriage didn't last forever. I have learned many dramatic lessons in domestic economy since the separation. Now I know why my mother used an old shirt to wash the kitchen floor. The buttons are brilliant for dislodging calcified cat food. If shirt manufacturers got their act together, they could quadruple their sales.

"Shirts specially designed for the separated male who has got all sorts of stuff stuck to his kitchen floor. Each shirt comes complete with an attachable scrubbing brush which clips neatly onto the tail."

I am no longer surprised by the number of alien socks which I find in my hot press. Socks which I have certainly never bought myself. I discovered a woman's bra last week which definitely does not belong to anybody that I know. I think it happens at the launderette. A sort of redistribution of clothing takes place which is very exciting because you never know what you will find in your black plastic bag when you get home.

All the girls in our primary school did cookery classes. We were much too busy sawing wood and hammering nails to bother.

I'd love to know how many of the boys now spend half of their life on the phone ordering breast of chicken curry from the takeaway. I do.

We all did elocution lessons. I learned how to ask in a posh voice — "Are you copper-bottoming the boat sir?" And how to reply in the same plummy tones — "No — I'm aluminiuming it, mum." I have spent many long years wandering around boat-yards searching for an opportunity to ask somebody that question. To this day I have never met anybody who looks even remotely like he is copper-bottoming a boat. Or aluminiuming it either.

*

How About A Denture Pride Week?

The main trouble with dentures is that you can only take them out in private. The only people who don't run away shrieking when they see them are nurses and dentists. A nurse will valiantly stand her ground in the face of legions of top sets and bottom sets, even if they are lined up on a shelf and they're all grinning at her.

They're not the sort of thing you admire either. You'd never dream of saying "My word ... I'm just mad about your dentures... they really do suit you. How are they on apples and hard pears?" You can think it all right. That's no harm. But you should never go into rhapsodies about other people's false teeth. They won't thank you for it.

I believe that every restaurant worthy of the name should have a little button set into the floor for each diner. If you feel a sudden urgent need to whip out your dentures you simply press the button and that activates a discreet siren. Everyone hears it but nobody knows who pressed their button. That is exactly as it should be. Then everybody in the place closes their eyes and keeps them closed until the all-clear sounds. That gives you loads of time to remove grape pips before they open their eyes again. Proper order.

I think that we need to develop some sort of Denture Pride. Politicians, celebrities, society columnists, film stars and television presenters can give us the lead by announcing proudly ... "My dentures have given me a reason to start living again ... my goodness, how I wish you could see into my bathroom at night. It would gladden your heart. It certainly gladdens mine."

My own set has never leaped out and put the heart across innocent bystanders. But they have come dangerously close. After a while you realise which poems place your audience most at risk and you stand sideways on stage while you're performing them. That way, if the worst happens they will only fly into the wings.

You can buy tubes of stuff which works on the same principle as quick-setting putty. But many people will only ask for it in the chemist's when the shop is empty and there is nobody looking in through the window.

Perhaps we can be coaxed out into the open by special offers. Half-price admission to cinemas before six o'clock, free bus travel at off-peak, first refusal on World Cup tickets.

I think it's the very least we deserve. We don't be hearing from the Tooth Fairy again.

*

When The Clicking Has To Stop

My dentist didn't know. I asked a couple of priests. They hadn't got a clue either. I simply wanted to know the name of the patron saint of upper sets of dentures. I've never had anything remotely like them before. I wish to start each day from now on with a very fervent prayer. "Dear Patron Saint of Upper Dentures, I haven't got the faintest idea what keeps them up. Is it gravity or suction or what? Please look after me today. When I'm in the bank trying for a loan or asking my publisher for a few bob, please grant that they neither change position suddenly, click, rattle or hop out unexpectedly on the table, Amen."

My speech pattern has changed dramatically overnight. I've had to rethink my entire vocabulary and eliminate any words which start with the letter "S". Whenever I try to say them I do a sort of tuneless lisping whistle. I was on Howth Dart Station last week and was just about to ask for a "Single to Sydney Parade" when I stopped myself. I can't say that anymore. So I asked for a return to Connolly instead. I didn't want to go there but there's no "S" in it. I've been on loads of Dart stations for the first time in the past week. Dalkey is easier to say than Sandymount so I go there instead. "Yes" is gone for good. I now nod my head and say "Affirmative."

As far as I am aware nobody in the public eye has ever whistled, rattled or clicked in the middle of a speech. How do they do it? During the past week I have listened very closely to *Today in The Dail*. I have also studied videos of Ronald Reagan, Elizabeth Taylor, Bob Hope and *An Ceann Comhairle*. I can only conclude that they have either all got their own teeth or a very good dialogue coach. None of them would have the slightest problem going to Sydney Parade on a single ticket or singing "Shine up your buttons with Brasso."

*

Saints Be Praised

St. Joseph of Cupertino must dread this time of year. Right now he must feel like going into hiding. Leaving Cert students all over Ireland who have never opened a book are blitzing him with petitions and bribes and rash promises. "Dearest St. Joseph ...old friend ... hi! A bit of a miracle please. Not a really big one. A nice little one will do. Just get me through the next couple of weeks and I promise ... I'll never watch those videos again ... you know the ones I mean." He must be demented. There they are up in heaven. Little groups of ordinary saints all standing around on clouds. Not a bother on them. Talking about first-class relics and halos. "I can't do a thing with mine ... the darn thing keeps slipping. I just dread doing an apparition at the moment ... it's no joke flitting across the gable end of a church when any second you know that your halo is going to fall off." Meanwhile St. Joseph of Cupertino is working a 24 hour day in the Prayers Inwards section. A young guy from Sligo wants a nice easy question about Hamlet. A girl in Cork wants a guarantee that she won't get a panic attack in the middle of her Cubic Graphs. Everybody wants something. If you weren't a saint you could tell them all where to go. "Now listen brother, don't be bothering me with your honours history ... I'm supposed to be up here enjoying everlasting bliss, not listening to you raving on about points and tips and exam pressure."

St. Anthony loves this time of year. So does St. Jude. At last they can see somebody else under a bit of pressure. They never get a moment's peace. Every time somebody can't find their reading glasses they get St. Anthony out of his bed. The poor man is on call night and day to find nailfiles, front door keys and handbags. St. Jude is worse. That unfortunate saint has got responsibility for Impossible cases. He's on valium. For the next two weeks they can throttle back a bit and watch their pal being put to the pin of his halo by Leaving Cert pressure. "And don't

come complaining to us. Now you know how we feel. In a couple of weeks the exams will be over and you can go back to grooving around on clouds for the rest of the year. You don't know when you're well off-that's your trouble."
I think I'll be a nice ordinary saint with responsibility for bees and honey. Old ladies can keep my picture in their prayer books and whisper prayers at me. I think I can handle that. *Amen.*
*

And None Of Your Cut-Price Stuff Please

I was feeling very down last week. I really did need to lift my spirits so I stopped outside a jeweller's shop. Looking into the window and trying to find the most expensive watch on display. Every now and then I shook my head and spoke to myself — "£657...no way ...that's far too cheap. False economy. Buy a watch like that and you'd be lucky to get a year out of it." Already I was beginning to feel better about myself. "£986 ...no I don't think so ...I've had enough of this made in Taiwan stuff."   I wandered into the shop and asked to see the dearest watch that they had. I've spent too much of my life saying — "Have you not got anything cheaper?" I think that is where I fall down. I don't put a high enough price on myself. Now here I am standing inside a very up-market jeweller's shop inspecting a watch which retails at £11,995. I swear it. I even overcame the urge to ask, "How much will you give me off for cash?" I spend too much of my life asking that question too. It is a glorious feeling to stand in front of nearly £12,000 worth of watch and slowly shake your head. I don't think so. No offence or anything like that but it's a bit too much on the chunky side for me thanks very much. I bumped into a man outside the shop who asked me — "What's the story Pat?" So I told him. "The basic problem in this town is that you can't get a nice unchunky watch for £12,000." His solution was instant. "If I was you I'd go down to the Pound Shop."   The next jeweller's shop had a sterling silver toothpick in the window marked "£34". When you have just rejected a five-figure watch you really do feel — "My God — they're giving that away." So I rambled inside and asked to see something infinitely more expensive. The best they were able to manage was a nine-carat gold one which cost £140. It felt like such an anti-climax that I handed it straight back. I never knew that people used an object called a swizzle stick to take the bubbles out of their champagne. Now here I am inspecting a gold one which costs £175. "Ah no...no...it'd be fierce bad manners to wiggle a thing like that around in your glass." I also rejected a nine-carat cigar piercer for £145 because I couldn't bear to think of the agony that you'd inflict on the poor cigar. In the short space of about thirty minutes I had dismissed over £14,000 worth of gold and silver stuff. God — you feel great afterwards.

*

A Crisis For The Ceili Bands

It's easy for an orchestra. They watch the conductor and read their music and everybody stops playing at the same time. Nobody has any twiddley bits left over. But ceili bands are different. Everyone is belting away on their fiddles and some of them have reached 'Around The Kitchen And Don't Step On The Semi-Conscious Granny' while others are still blasting away at 'Maggots In The Minestrone'. The woman on the piano keeps playing the same binkedy bonk bit over and over again until everyone has safely reached 'Lord Kilfeather's Gallstones'. And that's the part where Nathan Quixby sensed a very real need. That's where they all began to play speculative diddle dee idles and optimistic snatches of' Biddy Brady's Bedlinen' until everyone found a bit where they could all stop together. "There's no problem in getting started," said Nathan Quixby to the World Commission on Consenting Ceili Bands. "Four bonks on the piano and you're all away on a hack." He even designated this 'Four Bonk Conditioned Response'. "Unfortunately," he con-

tinued, "there is no way of building in a corresponding Four
Bonk Stopping Signal without wrecking the spontanaeity."
And that was when he suggested a system of coded shouts.
"You can arrange this in advance with a reliable person at the
ceili. When they whoop 'Me life on ye Seanie' the band knows
that everyone should be lashing into 'Mattie Mangan's Nervous
Twitch'. A sudden yell of 'Your blood is worth bottling Bertie'
means throttle back a bit boys — one of the fiddlers is still
rampaging through 'Six Nights in a Haystack With Consolata
Gilligan's Second Cousin'." But it was pointed out to Quixby
that so many people get carried away and shout so many
different things at ceilis that one unexpected roar of 'Get up the
yard and take your piano with you' could cause musical chaos.
That was when Quixby hit on the notion of the Honda 50
motorbikes. Each member of the band sits up on a bike and
plays the fiddle while steering with their feet. They form up in
a perfectly straight line across a field while the pianist travels
alongside on the back of a lorry. A course is carefully measured
out with marker posts to indicate when the band should be
swinging out of their first reel and into the second. The course
ends with a sheer fiffty foot drop into a pit of bubbling volcanic
lava. "Unless you all flnish together lads someone is in for the
big drop," explained Quixby. The musicians indicated in a
secret ballot that they would rather take their chances with the
coded shouts. Quixby now wants them to practice playing their
music in a crouched position over six inch nails. "This is in case
you get to a venue and there are no chairs," he said. "It's called
The Ceili Crouch." The man has clearly got hidden depths.

*

A Mammy For Every Man

There is nothing sordid about these full-sized inflatable women.
They are specially designed for Irish men who have left home
and are living in flats or bedsitters. Men who miss the steadying
influence of the mother often seek a substitute. Now they can

have the world's very first inflatable mammy. Full sized, yet when the Mammy is deflated she can be carried around in the pocket. Ready for any emergency. She can be whipped out at any time and pumped up.

One of them appeared suddenly on a number 30 bus last week and when the conductor tried to collect a fare for it, the son explained that his mammy has the free travel. "If that yoke bursts," said the conductor, "it could blind somebody." So he took its name and address and submitted a written report. CIE has not yet fully decided where it stands on the inflatable mammy question. — "We have no objection to them travelling for nothing in their owner's pocket," said a spokesperson. "But once inflated, she must go underneath the stairs with the luggage. We don't want her exploding and putting the heart across the driver." Inflatable mammies are now standing in the corner of many Dublin bedsitters. They are fitted with a miniature voice box vhich can be pre-set by a time switch. If the door to the flat is opened after two o'clock in the morning, the mammy's eyes light up and she rasps: "Where were you till this hour, ye shameless pagan? Don't think I don't know what you were up to." If the son says something like "Aw mammy" — the voice is programmed to respond with: "Don't you 'aw mammy' me. What am I after rearin'? Will ye tell me that?" The inflatable mammy also incorporates a light-sensor which reacts to any sudden change in the atmosphere. If somebody dims the lights or switches them off altogether, the mammy glows bright green and sings 'Faith of Our Fathers'. A model is already in the planning stages which will react to the presence of a female in the room. The text for the voice box in this model has not yet been finalized. "Put one foot near the bedroom and I'll paralyse you." has been suggested. This of course is not suitable for one room bedsitters. "Remember what the nuns taught you and play scrabble for pennies," is the text most favoured.

The slightest trace of alcohol in the atmosphere activates a self-destruct mechanism in the rubber mammy. It begins to swell to an alarming size and a voice shrills: "Son — would ye be the cause of your mammy exploding and blowing herself to pieces?" The swelling can only be arrested by pouring the drink down the sink.

There is the ever-present danger of sons going home for the weekend and attempting to deflate their real mammies. This is something that Irish mothers must learn to live with.

*

If You Have A Pet You'll Want To Know This

It's widely accepted that after a while many persons who keep a pet start to resemble it in some way. Yet the growing body of evidence points in the other direction. It clearly indicates that pets take unto themselves many of their owners' characteristics. Amanda Verity-Squires agrees with this theory. She has a keenly developed sense of right and wrong. And she kept a pet rabbit. Every night she included it in her prayers: "God bless Twitcher and grant that he grows up to be an exemplary bunny." She knelt beside the cage and prayed daily for all rabbits everywhere, including the ones in Russia. The cage was always placed on top of the television during religious services. When Amanda went to Lourdes she discovered a shop which sold sweets containing holy water. On her arrival home she hollowed out carrots and embedded one sweet in each. The rabbit never knew the difference. One morning while Amanda was renewing the prayer wheels in her back garden, the rabbit escaped. It wandered off into the wild and was gradually accepted by the other rabbits.

Over the next few months an amazing phenomenon occurred. Whenever the wild rabbits raided somebody's vegetable garden, Amanda's pet was racked with guilt. It recalled those evenings on top of the television during 'Songs of Praise' and was tormented with remorse.

Very slowly this feeling communicated itself to the other rabbits. They formed an anguished circle and released their guilt feelings in the form of groans. Late that evening when the verger came to lock the parish church he found the rabbits groaning in the centre aisle. He crept up into the organ loft and softly played 'Abide With Me'. The rabbits went away happy. Even more startling proof is afforded by the case of Verity Gageby's sheep. She bottle-fed it as a lamb. One afternoon it watched as Verity's husband sawed the legs off the bed. He suffered from a pathological fear of heights. This profoundly affected the lamb. The following week it watched as local firemen talked Verity's husband down from a stepladder. The lamb was wide-eyed and trembling. Two years later it was grazing on a craggy cliff. Suddenly the trembling started again. Moments later the sheep overbalanced and hurtled downwards. A marquee in the grounds of the vicarage broke its fall and it shot through a stained glass window into the church on the rebound. At that precise moment the vicar was explaining how God's messages to mankind come in the form of subtle whispers. "That was when the bloody sheep crashed in through the window," he said afterwards.

This was not the same church where the rabbits groaned. It's important for you to know that.

*

Lust For Leather!

No right thinking person can condone his behaviour. It is nothing short of systematic torture. Somebody must be told. They're out there in the darkness every night. Their breath comes in shivery clouds. Groups of men in tracksuits and football boots. And the only thing any of them wants to do is kick a ball. Even a little kick will do. But the trainer won't allow it. "Yez have to be hungry for the ball," he tells them. "Yez have to really lust after that lump of leather, lads." He makes them lie on their backs and pedal imaginary bikes. He makes them sprint and hop and leap. "If I give yez the ball now lads yez won't fight for it on Sunday." All along the seafront in Dollymount are groups of grown men — ravenous for the ball. Some of them would kill with their bare hands for a glimpse of it. This is not a healthy situation. A bank official was walking home shortly before Christmas. After dark. Under his arm was a parcelled-up football for his eldest son. A present from Daddy and Mammy. He sensed that something was wrong when a group of men lying on their backs suddenly stopped pedalling imaginary bikes. Several of them sniffed the air. Their eyes widened. Nostrils dilated. "There's a ball somewhere in the offing lads!" one of them shouted. "Aw now lads," the trainer pleaded. "Stay on your backs and pedal them bikes." But he was too late. The lads broke rank and took off after the bank official. He got the fright of his life. Thirty men in tracksuits were hot on his heels — all shouting and roaring and bagsing the first kick. The bank official tossed his parcel in the air and shinned up a tree. "They ate it," he told a garda. "Me parcel ... they ate it - paper and all. They tore me football into shreds and devoured them. Then they ate the laces." These men were clearly much too hungry for the ball. The Football Association of Ireland are worried about this form of training. Too many teams are trotting out onto the pitch on Sundays in a dangerous state of frenzy. They haven't seen a ball for seven whole days. Their blood is up. More and more games are being abandoned shortly after the kick-off. The referee's report is brief and to the point. "Play suspended ... ball eaten." Some sports shops are now steeping their footballs overnight in drinking chocolate. This sort of carry-on should not be encouraged. It will only perpetuate the lust for leather and then where will we be?

Other Books Currently Available
From
Killeen Publications

The Madwoman Of Cork
& Other Poems
By
Patrick Galvin
£1.95
1-873548-07-9

Small Fat Boy Walking Backwards
by
Gerry Murphy
(Humorous Poems)
£5.99
1-873548-08-7

The Pocket History Of Cork
by
J. G. MacCarthy
£4.99
1-873548-32-X